GW00535698

The Essential Guide to Small Business Online Marketing

Matt Eve

Better Business Results
www.betterbusinessresults.com

For more information:

Better Business Results,
25, Straffan Gate, Straffan,
Co. Kildare, Ireland
Phone: Ireland +353 (0) 1 488 0985,
UK +44 (0)20 8242 4045
Email: info@betterbusinessresults.com
www.betterbusinessresults.com

This book is dedicated to my family. Thank you for all of the love and laughter. All I do is for you.

Matt

Contents

Preface

Most business owners are pretty good at *doing* the things their businesses are supposed to do, but not *marketing* them. They are even more perplexed when it comes to online marketing. If you are among them, then this book is for you.

Online marketing is more than designing a flashy website or listing your small business in a web directory. To make the most of what the internet can do for your business, you need to realise that online marketing operates on a different set of principles than its offline counterpart.

With dozens of books literally screaming at you in almost every bookstore you might ask "Why another book on online marketing?". A search for 'online marketing' on Amazon gives you more than 35,000 results. And add millions of web pages to that.

Well, this book proposes to be different from all of that. It intends to help you achieve better business results through smarter online marketing. The keywords here are 'better' and 'smarter'.

This book grew out of a web marketing program for small business owners on our site[1]. The program along with our other do-it-yourself marketing training courses on mobile marketing and social media generated huge enthusiasm.

The program on the site itself was a result of our yearning to do something for small businesses and entrepreneurs who have limited resources and hence were unable to afford to hire our online marketing services. We also came across passionate individuals who prefer to roll up their sleeves and do things themselves.

The courses we offered were typically one-day courses that teach mobile marketing and social media marketing strategies to effectively connect with a business's target audience and thus market its services.

---

[1] www.betterbusinessresults.com

The strategies discussed in the courses were the same as those we use for the clients who hire us to handle their online marketing programs. They are based on the proven 'done for you' marketing systems which helped hundreds of other businesses to improve their sales and profits.

The online courses were a huge hit and thousands of enthusiastic people accessed them. We received many mails describing how the strategies and systems described in the course helped them achieve better business results and improved their understanding of how online marketing works.

There are many reasons why we believe our strategies work better than other programs. First of all, we are different from a large proportion of other online marketing providers who profess to be 'different'. In their mad rush to be different from others, they create the so-called 'new business ideas and marketing strategies' which actually distract you from the rock-solid fundamentals of the business and communication that are timeless. We don't do that.

The principles of marketing have not changed but the way you take your marketing message to your prospects has. The tenets of consumer behaviour and human psychology have not changed but the way people interact with each other on the web did. We keep this in mind when we design our online marketing strategies.

This book has two purposes. One is to teach you how online marketing works in as simple a language as possible. And the other is to help you achieve better business results by making your online marketing effective. It will provide all the essential strategies you need to achieve your online marketing goals.

We believe that our online marketing approach is smarter because it takes into consideration that different businesses have different ways of functioning and are at different stages of evolution. Some might be small but well-entrenched in the market. Some are just starting up and have limited financial resources. And others are local businesses that want to improve their online presence.

Whether your primary objective is to increase online sales or improve online brand image, this book will tell you how to do that in easy-to-understand and step-by-step process. You will learn how to use various web channels available to achieve a range of marketing goals within challenged budgets.

If you already have online presence but want to learn how you can explore its full potential, then this book will teach you a lot of techniques and strategies necessary to make the maximum use of internet.

There are many businesses which pay top prices to build a flashy website but wonder why it doesn't attract any visitors. While their intentions are good, they fail in achieving their objectives because most of them view internet as a medium of being seen 'doing something' rather than use it as a new means to connect with their audience and present them with a new experience. This 'set it and forget it' approach no longer works. The new model of marketing is to engage your prospects and clients in an ongoing conversation.

This book will teach you how to take full advantage of various social media and marketing channels on the internet to communicate effectively, attract more customers, increase web traffic, make more sales and ultimately to achieve better business results through smarter online marketing strategies.

Matt Eve
matt@betterbusinessresults.com
www.betterbusinessresults.com

Chapter 1
An Introduction to Online Marketing

The internet has altered our lives in many ways. Social media has changed the way we communicate with each other. The rules of the new marketing are radically different from those we have been following till now. The way a business connects with its customers has undergone a revolutionary transformation. Now, online presence is more important than a real office and the traffic you generate is the new currency of power. Welcome to the wonderful world of online marketing and its unlimited possibilities.

The shift to online marketing

*If you are not doing business on the internet by the year 2000,
you won't be doing business.*

Bill Gates

Well, Bill Gates' prediction might have gone off the mark but he
has a point. Whether you are a plumber or the local dentist,
online marketing is something you cannot just do away with.
Nowadays, your online presence is perhaps more important than
offline presence.

Take a look at these statistics to know how people are using the
internet.

- More than 2 billion searches are performed daily on the
  internet.[1]
- Half the buyers search about a product or service before
  ordering it.[2]
- More than 80% of netizens actively search for a product
  or service they are about to buy.[3]
- According to Google, 20 percent of all searches are local
  searches.[4]
- Microsoft puts the share of local searches on Bing at 53
  percent.[5]
- There are more than 3 million internet users in Ireland.
  That's nearly 66% of the population.[6]
- Online advertising spend in Ireland is $65 million dollars,
  an increase of 27% over last year.[7]

What does this tell you? People no longer use phone books or
Golden pages but hit on the internet to find the information they

---

[1] http://www.comscore.com/Press_Events/Press_Releases/2007/10/Worldwide_Se
arches_Reach_61_Billion/%28language%29/eng-US
[2] comScore, Inc. "March 2008 U.S. Search Engine Rankings." April 15, 2008
[3] comScore, Inc. "March 2008 U.S. Search Engine Rankings." April 15, 2008
[4] https://sites.google.com/a/pressatgoogle.com/googleplaces/metrics
[5] http://www.bizreport.com/2010/11/microsoft-half-of-mobile-searches-have-a-
local-intent.html
[6] http://www.internetworldstats.com/eu/ie.htm
[7] www.iia.ie/resources/download/59/

need. A large number of your would-be customers are trying to find you – *on the web*. And if you don't show up there then you are losing a lot of money.

The old ways of communication small businesses used to rely on do not guarantee that their message reaches the intended customer. Companies - small and large, local and global - are increasingly losing confidence in the traditional marketing media. Their focus is rapidly shifting to online marketing.

The traditional methods of marketing and advertising, such as television advertising and print media advertising basically try to interrupt users from what they were doing (watching sitcoms or reading news) and try to get their attention.

On the other hand people who are interested in you are actively trying to find you on the web. Getting found by them is more important than trying to reach them. No wonder online marketing spend is set to increase from $23 billion to almost $55 billion by the year 2014.[1]

How online marketing is changing the way we do business

The advent of the internet has brought a tectonic shift in the way we do business. The instantaneous transfer of information, ease of interconnectivity and elimination of middlemen along with the level playing field it offers to big and small players changed the business world in ways unforeseen.

New media is the new way of doing business. In fact, many businesses exist only on the net. As technologies evolve, the importance of new media can only increase further. Any business ignoring these radical changes will not only be ignored but also risk its very own survival. Those businesses which understand these changes and adapt to them will live on to tell the tale and have greater chances of flourishing in the information age.

---

[1] http://www.brafton.com/news/companies-continue-shift-from-traditional-online-marketing-1293309

How is online marketing different from offline marketing?

Traditional marketing is mostly advertising. It is a one-way communication flowing from the company to the consumer. There is no interactivity. All advertising depends on capturing the attention of the consumer with flashy and appealing images, messages and videos.

On the other hand, online marketing moves beyond the advertising paradigm. It is all about engaging and interacting with consumers. Communication is more direct and personal. You let the people participate in the conversation rather than dump your propaganda on their heads.

Traditional media rely on third party organisations such as television channels and newspapers to deliver their message. Online marketing lets you communicate with your audience directly without having to depend on other intermediaries.

Offline communication is one-way. But on the web, you not only interact with your customers but the customers can also interact with and among themselves.

The old way of advertising is based on designing marketing messages to be consumed by masses and released en masse. On the other hand, online marketing lets you target just the kind of audience you need. You can deliver the message at precisely the moment your consumers need it.

Offline marketing is all about reaching your customers. Online marketing is about reaching your customers as well as getting found by them. To capture space in the minds of consumers, organisations need to have inflated budgets in the case of traditional marketing. To the contrary, even small businesses can build a strong brand image through online marketing. It's all about being smart and creative rather than having big bucks.

Then there are things that never change

While online marketing is revolutionary and offers almost unlimited possibilities, do not get carried away by the hype. Whether you market your business online or offline, there are some fundamentals of marketing that never change and are timeless.

First of all, you need to have a clear idea of what business you are in and what it is that you are trying to sell. You need to know your product. You have to be able to convince the audience that it is in their interest to buy your product or order your service.

The psychological processes that go on inside the heads of customers that lead them to make a 'buy' decision are the same, whether offline or online. Without substance and clarity in your marketing message you will not be able to make an impression with your customers.

Spin might work for some time in the offline world but on the web, people look for authenticity. Remember that bad word spreads just as fast good word on the web. A mediocre website with great customer service attracts more customers and wins more business over the time than a flashy website with poor customer experience.

Great content that clearly explains the intended message and motivates the customers to make the choice you want them to make is the key to the success of any marketing campaign in both offline and online marketing.

What you say and how you say it is more important than the media you use to say it. In fact, online marketing is more about creating conversations and building communities than delivering messages.

The way you differentiate yourself from your competitors, how you project your product or service, your ability to give a positive experience to consumers instead of merely trying to grab their attention is something you need to focus on.

Knowing your target audience clearly is the parameter that determines your success on the online world. All the SEO (Search Engine Optimisation) techniques, web designing excellence and other gizmo stuff come later.

How you can be left behind if you are not using online marketing

There might be many businesses which do not have a web presence but they risk missing a spectrum of powerful tools and platforms offered by internet and online marketing. Almost all businesses, no matter what kind of products and services they offer, can benefit by online marketing.

Think about it. 66% of people in Ireland use the internet. More than 80% of them use the net to gather information just about anything they want to buy. Social networking sites have a penetration rate of 84.2% in Ireland.[1] Would you still want to miss them?

Even if you decide not to engage your customers online, your competitors won't sit still. According to a survey by the internet consultancy firm AMAS[2]; print advertising is fast losing out to online advertisement across a range of digital channels in Ireland. Social media has become an established part of marketing armoury of Irish marketers.

The survey[3] also reveals that 84% of marketers use social media to build better relationships with their customers, 76% use it to create better brand awareness and 66% use it to monitor conversations about companies, brands and people.

Without a smart online presence you will miss the customers who are trying to reach you and know about your products and services. You miss opportunities to understand them, to listen to their opinions and to socialise with them.

---

[1] comScore 2010 Europe Digital Year in Review
[2] 2011 Irish Online Marketing Sentiment Survey, AMAS
[3] 2011 Irish Online Marketing Sentiment Survey, AMAS

The 'loss of opportunity' costs of your digital invisibility far outweigh any tangible loss of your existing business. If you are a small business owner with no online presence then it is time you get moving in that direction before you get left behind by your competitors.

Here are some reasons why you need to embrace online marketing –

- Online marketing is not just for big boys. The internet is a great level playing field that offers boundless opportunities to businesses, both small and big.
- It's all about niche ideas and niche marketing. The long tail of the internet refers to the traffic that small sites attract by catering to the needs of a small group of people.
- Online marketing is very inexpensive when compared to traditional marketing. If you have a knack of understanding internet concepts then you can even do it on your own.
- The low start-up and maintenance costs let you play against competitors of any size. On the web, the guy with the smarter ideas usually wins rather than the one with the biggest budget.
- A strong online presence helps you to get found by your customers who would otherwise not know of your services.
- Creating a 5-star website is far less expensive than renting a 5-star office. An impressive online presence attracts customers easily and is an economic way to generate income.
- Depending on the type of products you sell and services you offer, the internet allows even a small business to go global.
- Digitally downloadable products such as software, music, movies, and eBooks and services that can be performed over the internet such as transcription, customer support, and writing and translation services can be sold via the internet with no geographic and time zone restrictions. Some of them even go almost exponentially.
- Even if you are a local business offering services that can only be consumed locally, the internet lets you attract au-

diences, whether local or global, to your site and monetize the local search traffic relevant to your business in a very cost-effective way. It extends your existing customer catchment area.

- Online marketing expands your geographic reach and market. It puts you just one click away from your customer. The tools and technologies offered by online marketing help you get to know your competition, foster customer loyalty, deliver better customer service and thus create a loyal fan base.
- Last but not the least, change is inevitable. If you don't change you get left behind beneath the merciless sands of time.

Goals of small business online marketing

Some clever online entrepreneurs look at the internet not just as a marketing medium but as a business habitat – the very place where products and services are conceived, created, marketed and sold. While such a business model is not viable for all kinds of business, organisations can use the internet in many other ways to achieve a range of goals.

Two of the most important goals of any online marketing program are –

1. **To increase online sales**. This is achieved via spreading the word among your targeted audience about your online presence, increasing inbound traffic and converting those visitors into buyers through skilful persuasion.
2. **To increase contact-to-purchase calls.** Not all products and services can be sold online. But by providing the necessary information your prospects need and by delivering a positive brand experience you can motivate them to contact you online or offline with a strong purchasing intent.

How to achieve better business results through smarter online marketing

To achieve your online marketing goals you need to realise that flashy websites and mere traffic are not enough. You need to be a lot smarter than that. Marketing is not advertising. It is a process of developing value and communicating it to your prospects.

As discussed earlier, some marketing fundamentals never change. Without a clear idea of what it is you are trying to achieve online and what value your product or service proposes to the customer, spending money on online marketing will not take you far.

Before conceiving your online marketing strategy, you need to do some soul searching. You need to be honest and think hard and deep. Without stating obvious answers and jumping to premature conclusions, you need to redefine your business, your audience and your marketing message. The following questions might help you.

- **What are you trying to accomplish?** We know that you want more sales and more profits but that is not a very helpful answer. You need to be more specific than that. You need to focus on outcomes rather than outputs. What value do you want to propose? What is the purpose of your campaign? To increase online orders or to increase brand awareness? What message do you want to communicate? What experience do you want to give to your prospects?
- **Who are your audience?** Do you really know them? What is their decision-making mechanism? How can you use online marketing to specifically target various stages in that purchase decision-making cycle? How do you identify your audience from any other guy surfing the net? Where do they live? What do they watch and listen to? How can you package your service so as to make them want to buy it?
- **What is your message?** What valuable information do you offer that is important to your audience? What makes your service so special? What makes you the authority of

information that makes people come to you and believe you? Is your message designed just to grab attention or to provide an experience? Does it bond with your audience? Is it a one-way communication or a sincere attempt to initiate a conversation?

The BBR approach to online marketing

At BBR (www.betterbusinessresults.com), we believe that technology is a means to an end rather than an end in itself. Simply using online tools for the sake of using them will not produce the results you have been looking for. The success to online marketing is not just in understanding the 'online' part but also in the 'marketing' part.

The marketing strategy of any business is still guided and determined by 4 Ps – Product, Price, Placement and Promotion. To achieve lasting success both offline and online, you need to have a deep understanding of your product, pricing strategy, placement in the market and its promotion.

BBR literally grew up with digital and social media revolution ushered by the web 2.0. Our vast experience with hundreds of small and medium businesses in digital marketing not only reinforced our beliefs in the ground rules of marketing but also taught us how the web is creating fundamental shifts in these 4 Ps.

Products. The internet can help you involve your customers with your business right from the product design stage. It lets you customize your products according to the needs and wishes of the customers. For example, Nike (www.nike.com) allows customers to design their own sport shoes.

Well, this may not be relevant to every product and service but the interactive nature of the web lets you get involved closely with your customers and hear what they have to say in ways that are not possible in the offline world.

Figure 1.1 The 4 Ps of Marketing Strategy

There are also a range of digital products such as software, music, and other downloadable information-based products which owe their existence solely to the internet. If your business creates such products and services, then the internet can be a very valuable tool in developing products to the specification of your customers.

Unlike the offline world, the internet is not dominated by a few big players. People on the net are looking for niche products and customised services as evident from the long tail of internet marketing. There is a fundamental shift from mainstream products to much smaller niche products and services. Online marketing helps you to identify such markets and create products that appeal to them.

Price. With the proliferation of shopping price comparison websites it has become very easy for customers to compare the prices of competing products with just a mouse click. Such intense competition usually drives down the prices.

On the other hand, smart online marketing lets you build a base of loyal customers to whom you can up-sell and cross-sell relevant products for a premium. Using various social media, you can understand what your customers really want and then tailor your offerings to their specifications.

Placement. The internet expands your geographic reach. Through intelligent online marketing you can advertise your products and services on a global scale. For digitally downloadable products there is almost no limit as to how far they can go.

Hundreds and thousands of small businesses flourish on the internet using the mail order marketing model. They benefit from a larger customer base and wider geographic reach within the limits imposed by banking and shipping restrictions.

Promotion. This is the most influenced aspect of the 4 Ps with the advent of online marketing. As discussed before, online marketing lets you reach your target audience in a very cost-effective way when compared to traditional promotional media.

On the web, there is no limit to how many conversations you can have with your customers. The messages can be personalised in ways unforeseen. The interactive environment offered by the net can help you reach a global audience and build loyal communities. Online marketing makes it very easy to target, track and measure your promotional campaigns with more accuracy than is possible in offline marketing. This vastly increases the effectiveness of your marketing efforts.

At BBR, we first take a deep look at the client's business needs and marketing goals. Then we analyse how various online tools and techniques can be used at every stage of the marketing cycle to achieve better business results. Our online marketing strategy formulation mechanism follows a rigorous approach to generate smart strategies that produce better business results.

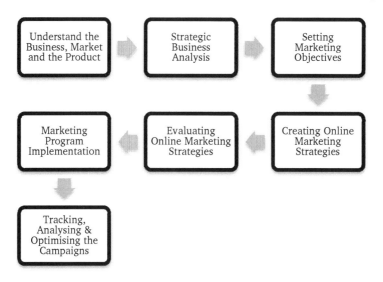

Figure 1.2 Creating an Online Marketing Strategy

1. **Understanding the Business Fundamentals.** No strategy can be effective unless it is deeply rooted in the fundamentals of the business. What exactly does your organisation strive to do in the marketplace? Who are your customers? What are their needs and how do you fill them? How does the internet affect the context of the business you operate in?

2. **Strategic Business Analysis.** Strategy is not something that is aimed at inanimate objects. It takes into account the presence of competitors, demands of the customers, availability of substitute products and things like that. A deep strategic analysis of the business presents us with useful insights that help you in formulating an effective marketing strategy.

3. **Setting Marketing Objectives.** Depending on the resulting conclusions of the analysis, you need to set SMART (Specific, Measurable, Achievable, Realistic and Time-bound) marketing goals. You also need to define the specific outcomes to know whether you have been able to achieve your goals.

4. **Creating Online Marketing Strategies.** Strategies need to be in sync with objectives. They need to have the right

marketing mix. A paid advertising campaign to increase traffic may significantly differ from one that aims to build a community using social media.

5. **Evaluating the Strategy.** Will this strategy be able to achieve its intended outcomes? What specific tactics do we need to adapt to make the campaign more effective? How does it address the short term objectives, long term goals and the ROI issues? Can it be implemented within the specified budget? By evaluating the strategy you get to know its strengths, weaknesses and the opportunities to refine it.

6. **Executing the Strategy.** A lot of firms go gung-ho about this stage but the results are invariably determined by what happens prior to execution. A lot of online marketing techniques are the same but only a few achieve the right results. That is because, though they use the same tactics, it is the strategies that make the difference.

7. **Tracking, Analysing and Optimising Campaigns.** Online marketing tools let you track where your campaign is going with more meticulous detail than is possible in the offline marketing. The response of the customers can be known almost instantaneously and that lets you tweak the campaign to suit the evolving needs. This feedback loop allows you to make the necessary course-corrections with amazing effectiveness.

A smart process to achieve better business results

By using a spectrum of online marketing tools such as email marketing, paid search marketing, search engine optimisation, affiliate marketing, viral marketing, social media, mobile marketing, web PR, online relationship management and other marketing platforms, BBR creates the right marketing mix that is most relevant to your marketing objectives.

Businesses that offer services that can only be consumed locally have different needs. By using smart phone ads and locally-directed paid advertising, traffic can be increased to achieve better business results. Using a range of social networking sites large number of relevant visitors can be directed to your website. Paid advertising such as banner ads, PPC (pay per click) and affiliate marketing ads are used to attract customers.

By making use of smartly designed targeted landing pages, better conversion rates can be achieved. Using diverse forms of information platforms such as web content, blogs, forums and videos, better lead-to-buyer ratios can be achieved.

BBR online marketing process focuses on immediate revenue growth as well as long term business growth. All information of prospects and customers is saved and categorised to gain insights into their buying habits. Using mobile short codes and SMS follow-ups any new offers and discounts are immediately conveyed to the relevant customers.

Using rich content, customers are kept in touch through Face-Book, email newsletters, webinars, white papers and mobile app content. The highly valuable customer database can also be profiled to follow them up offline through postcards, newsletters and other printed material.

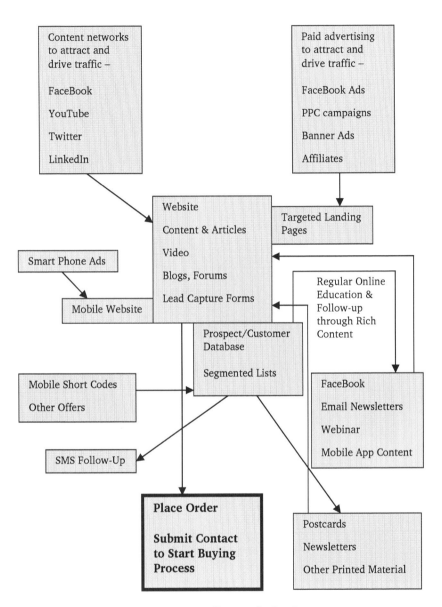

Figure 1.3 BBR Online Marketing Process

Chapter 2
Understanding Online Marketing

The success of any online marketing program rests on two things – traffic and conversion. Traffic is the life-blood of any marketing campaign and you need to attract as much relevant traffic as possible through a suite of organic and paid search marketing techniques. Then using hypnotic content that gains prospects' confidence, you motivate them to make a 'buy' decision and turn them into buyers. Understand that relevant traffic and appealing content are what determine who you are online.

Understanding the components of online marketing

Online marketing is very broad in scope and refers to all kinds of marketing activities performed over not only internet but also other wireless media such as mobile telephones. Here are some of the most commonly used online marketing tools –

- Search Engine Marketing
- Search Engine Optimisation
- Pay-Per-Click (PPC) Advertising
- Email marketing
- Article Submission & Syndication
- Social Networking
- Social Bookmarking
- Affiliate Marketing
- Mobile Marketing
- Web PR
- Online Video Marketing
- Blogs, Microblogs and Forums
- Viral Marketing

Whatever the suite of tools and technologies you select, all online marketing campaigns have two important aspects - generating web traffic to your site and converting the visitors into buyers. Let us see what these online marketing tools mean, how they work and in what way can they be used in promoting your business.

Search engine marketing

People all over the world use search engines such as Google[1], Yahoo![2], Bing[3] and other sites to find the information they are looking for. These search engines index the web and use complex algorithms to display results based on the queries (called keywords) typed by the users.

---

[1] www.google.com
[2] www.yahoo.com
[3] www.bing.com

The results displayed by the search engine (SERP or Search Engine Results Page) mean a lot to businesses. A top rank on a search engine for the keywords relevant to your business can help make millions of Euros. Most people consider, often incorrectly, that the number one position on an SERP is the Holy Grail of search engine marketing.

Search engine marketing is important because nearly 90% of all internet activity begins with search. Even when they know the name of the website they are looking for most people prefer to search for it in a search engine than type the URL in the address bar of the browser.

Search is also important because it is goal-oriented. When a user types a keyword, he or she is signalling an active interest. This helps you identify the kind of prospects you need and target them with various marketing tools.

Searches let you know the state of the mind of the customer. By analysing the search terms you can better understand the stage of the buying cycle the customer is in. This allows you to target them using a more appropriate marketing message.

The search industry is huge. According to comScore[1], more than 18 billion searches were conducted in the April of 2011 in US alone. Google is the world's most used search engine with an unassailable market share of 91% followed by Yahoo! with 4% and Bing with 3%[2].

Research into internet browsing habits reveals that 84% of people do not go past the bottom of page two into the Google search engine results[3]. Having your website come up in the top ten results on the first page is like having a shop at the front door of the world's largest shopping mall. No wonder businesses spend so much to have their web site placed on the top of the SERPs. There is a whole discipline of online marketing called Search Engine

[1] http://www.comscore.com/Press_Events/Press_Releases/2011/5/comScore_Releases_April_2011_U.S._Search_Engine_Rankings
[2] http://gs.statcounter.com/#search_engine-ww-monthly-201010-201012
[3] http://www.gloctech.com/website-development/search-engine-optimization.html

Optimisation (SEO) that aims to make your web pages top the organic searches.

As said earlier, the internet is not just for the big boys. Depending on who you listen to, local search (searches related to specific products and services offered in specific locations such as 'hair salon Dublin') accounts anywhere from 20 percent to 53 percent in the total search volume. And that is so huge that anybody ignoring it would be making a foolhardy business decision.

So how do you come up on the top of search engine results page? There are two types of search results displayed by the search engines. The first type is organic results which are the results produced naturally by the algorithm of the search engine. Since these are not influenced by advertising revenue and financial payments, they are natural and have more authenticity and credibility with users.

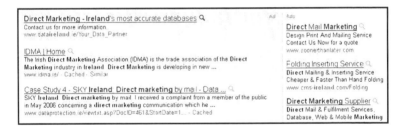

Figure 2.1 Organic and Sponsored Results

On the other hand, paid search results can be bought by advertisers through bidding. They are usually displayed at the top and the right of the organic results so as to distinguish them from natural results. Paid search marketing is also known as PPC (pay per click) advertising as you pay only when a web user clicks on your ad.

While organic search results are important to build authority in cyberspace and sustained brand leadership, it is usually paid results that help you in making quick money. So you need an intelligent mix of both SEO (to have better organic search results) and PPC (to attract more traffic through paid search results).

SEO and PPC use different approaches to generate traffic to your website. Both have advantages and disadvantages that you must carefully consider before pouring your valuable financial resources into them.

Organic Search Marketing	Paid Search Marketing
These marketing campaigns have long gestation periods & it may take months to see any monetary benefits. But the effect produces long-term ROI.	Paid search marketing produces effects within days and weeks. But the effect usually wears off faster than organic search.
Organic results have greater visibility and carry more authenticity.	Paid search results have less visibility and elicit less trust when compared to organic results.
It takes time and effort to reach to top rankings on organic search results.	It is easy to reach top position. All you need to do is to bid high.
Cost of marketing campaigns is comparatively low.	Paid search marketing can be expensive depending on the competition for keywords.
It is very useful in creating more awareness, exposure and branding.	Paid search marketing is not that helpful in long term brand awareness and community building.

This book will teach you how to avoid the hyper-emphasis on number one rankings on the SERPs and other traps of search engine marketing. It will instead focus on attracting relevant traffic and using great content to achieve better conversion rates with particular emphasis on marketing small businesses on the net.

SEO – Search Engine Optimisation

Search engine optimisation aims to optimise your web site so that it achieves a top rank on the search engine results page. The nature and practice of SEO is invariably determined by the way search engine algorithms rank the web pages. As search engines sites such as Google and Bing continue to make changes in their algorithms, the techniques used in SEO keep changing.

There are many factors that influence the ranking of a web page on an SERP. To get a top rank, your web page needs to be relevant to the keywords typed in the query, provide important information related to the query, be popular on the web and elicit trust and authority on the related subject.

SEO tries to optimise your web pages using a range of techniques and strategies but most of them fall into the following five categories –

Designing Search Engine Friendly Web Site

To be searched by search engines you first need to be indexed by the web crawlers. SEO tries to make web pages more search engine friendly by making use of appropriately titled web pages, easily index-able file directories, relevantly titles images, videos and flash ads and an effective navigation system.

Using Relevant Key Phrases

A web site can only be optimised for so many key phrases and you need to choose them with care and only after thorough testing. Selecting the right keywords is the key to success of any SEO as well as PPC campaign. You need to think of the key phrases that your prospects might be using to find products, services and information your business provides.

You also need to be careful about the keywords to which you wish to optimise your site for, especially when you are a local business. For example, if you sell used agricultural equipment in county Meath, you should perhaps optimise your web site for the keywords 'used agricultural equipment + Meath' instead of plain 'used agricultural equipment' as the later can mean any company all over the world selling agricultural equipment.

Since search engines rank the web pages according to the optimal presence of key phrases typed in the query, SEO tries to enhance the content on your web pages with the relevant keywords that are meaningful to your marketing campaign.

By using keywords in the title tags, HTML meta-tags and in the content on the web pages, it is possible to improve the ranking on the search engine results page. However, many search engines penalise for overstuffing of keywords in web pages. So this is something your SEO campaign needs to keep in mind.

Choosing keywords is not as easy as it seems. A lot of thinking needs to put into the search psychology of your targeted audience. Search volume, competition for keywords, their relevance to your business and the ease of convertibility of the keywords are few things you need to work on.

There are keyword suggestion tools available online that can be very useful in arriving at the most relevant ones that help you achieve better business results. We will discuss how to choose the right keywords in a later section.

Keyword Optimised Content

Content is still the king. The best web sites on the web are usually the simplest ones. Think of Amazon[1]. Instead of flashy web design, they focus on providing rich content that attracts visitors time and again. To attract more traffic and achieve higher search engine rankings, you need to create quality content that is optimised with the right set of relevant keywords.

Great content provides useful information to visitors. It engages them and makes come back to you. It convinces prospects and motivates them to make a buying decision. When you keep providing such content to your visitors, over time you become an authority in that particular topic and begin to elicit high amount of trust and authenticity. That creates unassailable long term growth.

Keyword-optimised content contains an appropriate title tag, H1 header tags, body content of at least 350 words (but not more than 900) that is split into easily digestible chunks with relevant sub-headings and a keyword-containing URL. Through suitable meta-description, link anchor texts, image

---

[1] www.amazon.com

and video anchor texts content can be made more SEO-
friendly.

Increasing Link Popularity

Search engines give better rank to the web pages which are
linked to other relevant web pages. The more referrals you
have through links pointing to your site the better your rank
will be. A large proportion of SEO effort is taken up by creating more backlinks to improve popularity on the web and
hence increase its search engine ranking.

All links are not created equal. The quality, relevance and the
page ranks of the links pointing to your page is a more accurate determinant of your search engine ranking. A web page
with few high quality backlinks is more likely to come up top
on SERP than the one with more but less quality backlinks.

SEO uses many techniques to improve link popularity. The
most popular and effective technique is to create excellent
content that people want to read, talk about and link back to.

Creating interesting viral content such as articles, videos,
downloadable software applications, eBooks, games, white
papers, reports and other free giveaways which people want
to use and share among their online friends is a sure fire way
to gain more links and improve page rank.

Localised and Personalised Search Optimisation

Search engines try to generate increasingly relevant search results to their users by taking into consideration their geographic and personal preferences. This is to be expected as a
significant proportion of searches are local searches. Studies
also show that people use the same keywords they used a
while ago to revisit and re-read information.

This aspect of SEO is also the most relevant one to many
small and medium businesses. By optimising your chosen
keywords along with your locality you would be better able to
generate more relevant traffic.

PPC advertising

Pay per click is a form of advertising where the advertiser pays only when a user clicks on the advertisement which is displayed a sponsored result along with the organic search results for various search terms. First created and popularised by Google[1], the PPC model of advertising revolutionised the online industry.

In this system, the advertiser needs to select the keywords to which the advertisement is aligned with. This means when a user searches using the keywords you have identified, your result will be displayed as a sponsored result. Choosing the right keywords is the key to the success of a PPC campaign.

Advertisers need to bid for keywords. The fiercer the competition the more you need to pay. Since search engines display only a limited number of sponsored results, advertisers compete amongst each other for the top spot. Bidding wars for some keywords can drastically shoot up your PPC campaign costs.

The advertisement can only be four lines with the first line being a headline and the last line a display URL. The headline cannot exceed 25 characters and the display URL can only be 35 characters long. That leaves just two lines with a combined maximum limit of 70 characters.

Ireland Florist & Flowers 🔍
Fresh Irish Flowers Hand Delivered
Order by 12pm for same day service
www.teleflorist.ie/Flower+Delivery+Ireland

Figure 2.2 An Example of a PPC Advert

So you need to be creative in designing ads to make an impact. Better results can be achieved by using relevant headlines, focussing on USP of the product or service, offering freebies and including a strong call to action that motivates people to click on your advertisement.

---

[1] http://adwords.google.com

Email marketing

Email marketing is the online equivalent of the direct marketing, which can be put to great effect both as a marketing platform and as an online relationship management tool. It is very cost-effective, customisable on a large scale, easily measurable and can be highly targeted.

Marketing emails can be promotional or retention-based. Promotional emails are designed to elicit interest in the buyer about a particular product or service and try to increase their purchase intent.

On the other hand, retention-based emails are mails designed to provide useful information to the recipients and build long term relationship with them. This kind of education based marketing can be very effective for more complex products and services which typically have a longer buying lifecycle. By regularly sending educational content the objective is that you both educate your prospects and also demonstrate your expertise which makes you stand out from your competitors. These emails may also include promotional messages but they are mostly used for relationship building purposes.

Like direct marketing mails, email marketing is often overused. The menace of spam is taking the sting out of email marketing. Email deliverability and mail bounce are two biggest issues in email marketing. You need to make sure that any promotional email you send adheres to the Directive of Privacy and Electronic Communications (DPEC)[1] which is in force in all EU countries.

The success of email marketing is mainly determined by the quality of email recipient lists. Opt-in lists (emails whose owners have given explicit permission to send them promotional emails) work better than general email databases.

Email marketing can be put to great effect in fostering long term relationship with your customers. By using email opt-in forms and

---

[1] http://eur-lex.europa.eu/LexUriServ/LexUriServ.do?uri=CELEX:32002L0058:EN:HTML

offering freebies on your web site you can collect and create a high quality database of potential customers.

Using advanced software programs, email marketing campaigns can be measured and analysed to their finest detail. Many online marketers believe that email marketing is next only to search marketing in achieving high returns on investment.

A cleaning products supplier came to us looking for a way to keep his existing customers up to date with his ever expanding product range and to encourage them to try out other products.

We devised an electronic email newsletter that goes out monthly to all his customers. In addition we created a hard copy newsletter that goes out every other month. Both of these newsletters include tips and case studies of new products available and how to use them.

In the first 8 months of implementing these customer retention systems turnover has increased by about 24%. In addition to introducing new products to his customers he has enjoyed increased sales of his existing product range.

As can be seen from this experience, customer retention pays a lot. You can up-sell and cross-sell to your existing customers. There is a fortune waiting to be mined from them.

Article submission & syndication

Article submission and syndication involves writing articles with useful and interesting content and then submitting them to various online article directories. Anyone can view, download and repost those articles on their web sites or blogs.

Those who repost your articles are required to include the 'about the author' section at the end of the article. This section contains an URL linking back to your web site or blog. As your articles spread on the net the number of backlinks pointing to your web site will increase. This helps to improve your link popularity and as a result your search engine page rank.

When you intelligently optimise these articles to your chosen keywords, it helps to improve the relevance of your web pages in the search engine results. Remember to post your articles on your site first and then post it on syndication portals.

When the articles contain useful and relevant information, they naturally attract a lot of backlinks as well as traffic. Users actively following such articles are more likely to buy related products and services.

The other benefit of article syndication is that it helps you promote yourself online and build a positive brand image. As more and more people follow you and your articles online, you become an authority on the subject and what you say elicits more trust.

However, article submission can produce poor results when the articles you post are of inferior quality. The web is filled with a lot of such trash and you need to either sharpen up your writing skills or hire professional writers to do the job.

Social networking

Social networking sites are services that let users share their interests and activities with other users and build relationships and communities. FaceBook[1], MySpace[2], Twitter[3], Orkut[4], LinkedIn[5], Hi5[6], and Habbo[7] are some of the most popular social networking sites.

Any interested web user can create a personal profile on these sites and share links, messages, videos, photos and other stuff with like-minded people across political, economic and geographic boundaries.

---

[1] www.FaceBook.com
[2] www.myspace.com
[3] www.twitter.com
[4] www.orkut.com
[5] www.linkedin.com
[6] www.hi5.com
[7] www.habbo.com

The personal profiles of social networking users can offer interesting and valuable insights to online marketers. You can identify the users who are in need of your products and services, recognize the target audience with more accuracy, understand the thought processes that go on in the minds of your likely prospects and use that information for your marketing purposes.

Social networking is second only to search on the list of most prominent activities web users spend time on[1]. Irish net users spend more than 18 hours every month on various social networking sites of which FaceBook tops the list, followed by various Google sites[2]. The reach of social networking sites in Ireland is 84.2% with a year-on-year growth of 8.1%[3] and this represents a huge market opportunity.

Social bookmarking

Social bookmarking sites allow people to bookmark online resources to store, organize, manage, search and share them with others. Users can tag the bookmarks, express their opinions and form groups with other like-minded people.

Some of the most popular social bookmarking sites on the web are delicious[4], digg[5], reddit[6], stumbleupon[7], technorati[8], dwellicious[9], socialmarker[10] and faves[11].

Social bookmarking is a useful tool in search engine optimisation as the more often a web page is bookmarked and tagged the more backlinks it has and hence a better search engine results ranking.

Social bookmarking also lets you find potential customers on the basis of bookmarking habits. You can create online communities

---

[1] comScore 2010 Europe Digital Year in Review
[2] comScore 2010 Europe Digital Year in Review
[3] comScore 2010 Europe Digital Year in Review
[4] www.delicious.com
[5] www.digg.com
[6] www.reddit.com
[7] www.stumbleupon.com
[8] www.technorati.com
[9] www.dwellicious.com
[10] www.socialmarker.com
[11] www.faves.com

about your products and services or provide useful information which you can use to soft sell your offerings. It is also a very important tool to build relationships with past and potential customers.

When a web page is tagged it creates a huge amount of traffic back to your site which you can use to improve your lead to sale conversion ratios. But bookmarking can also be a double-edged sword. If your service is poor or your products fail to deliver, the bad word spreads just as fast as any good things you might have to say about them.

Affiliate marketing

While SEO and social media marketing capture the lion's share of attention from the online marketers, affiliate marketing is a rather low profile tool that is often overlooked. But nevertheless, it is a very effective tool that can create wonderful results especially for small business online marketing.

In affiliate marketing you reward people (called affiliates) for bringing visitors or customers to your site through their own marketing efforts. The rewards are usually a fixed commission (called CPS – cost per sale) or a percent of sales (revenue sharing). Sometimes people are also rewarded just for bringing in traffic, irrespective of how many sales were achieved from their traffic.

Many small business owners prefer affiliate marketing because it is a 'pay per performance' model. Your affiliates bear the marketing costs and you pay them only for the results. Some online businesses like Amazon owe their initial success largely to affiliate marketing methods.

According to a marketing research experiment[1], if a small business can invest sufficient time and effort in creating strong affiliate programs, the returns on investment can far outweigh the returns from any PPC advertisement campaign over time. While affiliate marketing campaigns take time to build up momentum,

---

[1] http://www.marketingexperiments.com/ppc-seo-optimization/the-roi-on-ppc-vs.-affiliate-marketing.html

they typically have lower costs per conversion but higher returns than pay per click advertisement campaigns.

Mobile marketing

Mobile marketing refers to the use of mobile devices and networks by businesses to communicate with and engage their audience. Marketers use short codes, SMS, MMS, mobile web, in-game marketing, and mobile apps to promote their services.

Mobile marketing is a particularly useful tool for small local businesses as prospective customers can be identified and reached through various location-based services. The low marketing costs and increased sales due to increased response rates makes mobile marketing a must-use tool for small businesses.

> Dave, a bar owner, approached us looking for a way to keep in touch with his past customers and to let them know about special events happening at his bar.
>
> We devised a customer retention campaign for him where we created a system for capturing his customers' mobile phone numbers. Now whenever there is any kind of event, special promotion or arrival of a new brand Dave just lets us know and we send out a SMS message to all of his past customers.
>
> Feedback from Dave and his customers has been very positive. Customers like the non-intrusive way they can find out about events and Dave has an extremely cost effective way of filling his bar with paying customers. In fact, one of the recent SMS broadcasts we did for him yielded an amazing 16% response rate!

Mobile marketing in Ireland is growing at a rate of 5 percent every year and mobile advertising is set to reach 17 million Euros making up 1 percent of total advertising spend[1]. There are 5.2

---

[1] http://wirelessfederation.com/news/2134-mobile-marketing-accelerates-in-ireland/

million mobile phone users in Ireland and the mobile phone pene-tration is 121.5%[1]. With better handsets, 3G networks, interactive mobile TV and smartphone apps mobile marketing is set to reach even greater importance in the marketing mix.

Small businesses can use mobile marketing methods to keep in touch with their past customers and let them know about special events, discounts and announcements. It is also a great way retain your customers and boost repeat sales.

Visits to your web site via mobile phones are likely to be more purpose-driven and are more likely to be converted into a sale. Since mobile devices operate differently from a personal com-puter, the way web pages get accessed and viewed is significantly different.

To make mobile web browsing effective and to make full use of mobile marketing you need to have a separate website dedicated to people who are trying to access the site through mobile plat-forms.

Web PR

Public relations (PR) is the practice of managing public percep-tion of a person or a business using journalists and media houses. But with the advent of internet, businesses can now reach their audiences by bypassing traditional media though they still play an important role.

With social media occupying the central position on the web ac-tivities, the line separating marketing and PR is getting blurred. Press releases can be posted online and people get to know about them even before they appear in print.

There are a host of online press release directories you can use to make an announcement. If the message is appealing and has viral marketing value, it can bring a lot of traffic and highly motivated potential buyers to your site.

---

[1] http://www.comreg.ie/_fileupload/publications/ComReg0843.pdf

Press releases are not just for announcing big happenings. You can find or invent new reasons to post press releases regularly without overdoing it. By optimising the press releases with appropriate keywords you can also use them as an SEO tool.

Irish Press Releases (http://www.irishpressreleases.ie/) is the most popular free online PR directory in Ireland. Here are some of the most popular PR directories on the web.

> www.prweb.com
> www.24-7pressrelease.com
> www.1888pressrelease.com
> www.eworldwire.com
> www.pressreleasepoint.com
> www.clickpress.com
> www.pr.com
> www.i-newswire.com
> www.pressbuzz.com
> www.pressexposure.com
> www.pressbox.com

Online video marketing

The online video phenomenon is taking the net by storm and now videos viewed online exceed the number of search queries[1]. In many ways, online video is more effective than text and images in engaging audience because of the powerful mix of sight and sound.

Online videos are a great tool every small business must consider using to generate leads, improve sales and to communicate better in a more personal way. Further, videos are more viral than text based web pages and images. So people are more likely to share a video and talk about it than a primarily text-based web page.

Research also shows that online videos increase the time spent by the visitors on your site by at least 9% and boost conversion ratios[2]. It is also found that visitors who view videos are 85% more

---

[1] http://www.comscore.com/press/release.asp?press=2016
[2] http://www.internetretailer.com/2010/10/07/living-direct-raises-conversions-video-demos

likely to buy than visitors who do not[1]. Online videos are a powerful tool to increase the purchase intent of your customers and you must make full use of it.

Understand that posting videos is not just enough. Video SEO is slightly different from traditional search engine optimisation. Appropriate video metadata addition, page optimisation, thumbnails and play buttons to improve ease of use are few techniques to improve the page rank as well as the overall quality of the videos. We will explore more video SEO techniques in the later sections.

Blogs, microblogs and forums

Blogs are a type of website which allow users to publish their opinions on almost anything they like. While blog entries are mostly textual, bloggers (people who post blogs) can also post images, videos and audio podcasts. Almost all blogs allow readers to leave their comments and link back to other blogs, web sites and social networking sites.

If your web site does not have a blog then it's time you had one. Search engines give higher page ranks to web sites that provide regular fresh content over static ones. By starting a business blog you not only engage your audience with new useful content but also build long term relationships with them.

Another way you can use blogs is to find the bloggers who are popular in your market segment and approach them with juicy affiliate marketing opportunities or paid reviews for your offerings. When authoritative bloggers suggest a new product or service a lot of visitors buy the goods.

Microblogs are similar to blogs except that the blog entries are limited in length. For example, Twitter (www.twitter.com) limits its micro-blogging entries (called tweets) to 140 characters. Twitter is an effective way to get hundreds of people who are interested in your products and services to follow you with timely updates.

---

[1] http://www.internetretailer.com/2010/03/31/inside-search

Two types of people should be of interest to you on the Twitter – people who have lots of influence with many followers in your market segment and people who can be potential customers. Later on in this book, we will discuss various strategies that can be used to target both categories to advance your business interests.

Twitter can also be used to announce new offers, discounts and other sales promotions. Since people regularly follow their tweets, this tactic will produce more immediate results than posting the information about the same offers and discount sales on your web site or blog.

Forums are online discussion boards where users can post their opinions in the form of messages. While forums may not be relevant to all types of business they are a wonderful tool to build online communities by providing them with useful and interesting information and also to become a hub of relevant business discussions.

Viral marketing

Viral marketing is more a strategy than a tool. Since all tools need to be as viral as possible to produce their best result it needs special mention and explanation. To put it simply, viral marketing is just a buzz word for 'word of mouth' publicity.

To be more specific it involves making use of pre-existing online social networks to spread any information with overt or covert intention to promote your business interests such as more sales or increased brand awareness.

When people really like something on the net they tend to share it with their online friends. As their friends pass it further on to their friends the message keeps on spreading like a virus with near exponential rise.

But it is difficult to purposefully design a viral message and spread it around, as what makes a message viral is beyond the control of marketers. It's hard to guess what people will like in a message and even if they do it is unclear how we can monetise the effect. Of course, that does not lessen the importance of viral marketing.

The principles of viral marketing help us to maximise the returns of our online marketing efforts. By making our marketing messages more 'infectious' and 'virally marketable' we can boost their impact.

Some products and services are intrinsically more infectious than others but do not let that stop you from thinking up new possibilities.

- Give away free stuff. Make sure that it contains something valuable to your prospective customers. It could be an information-based product such as an eBook or white paper or simple discount coupons and codes.
- Spread the word. Use every means available to you, from emails to press releases, to make the message more popular.
- Be discreet and stop in-your-face advertising. People hate to be told what they need to buy. Focus on how to make the user's experience more exciting because experiences are infectious.
- Appeal to more senses. Text-based messages have less potential to be viral than videos and animations which engage more human senses and are likely to go viral.
- Make your offers shareable, downloadable and transferable. EBooks, audio and video files, embeddable HTML codes and RSS feeds are some examples which can be shared, downloaded and transferred. See how you can use these media to create a viral campaign.

Making the right online marketing choices

No matter what online marketing tool you use, the bottom line is that it has to be effective. There is no point in using a technique just for the heck of using it or because everybody is using it. Getting the right marketing mix depends on the objectives of the marketing campaign and the nature of the products being sold.

As discussed earlier, the fundamentals of marketing are same off-line as well as online. To make right choices in the marketing mix you need to have a clear idea of the 4 Ps of your business.

While the goals of the campaign and the tools used to achieve them may vary, almost all online marketing programs need to be effective in achieving the following objectives –

1. Generate relevant traffic
2. Capture leads
3. Engage customers by following up with rich content
4. Gain prospect's confidence to make the sale

Generating traffic

Traffic is the life blood of any online marketing campaign. All the time and toil you have put into building a quality site is of practically no value if no one visits to see it.

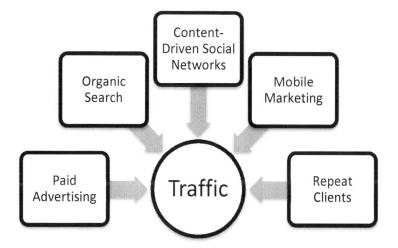

Figure 2.3 Five Important Factors that Affect Traffic

Like insurance policy selling, online marketing is a numbers game. You approach 100 people, 10 will click on the product page and 3 will buy it. More traffic means more leads and ultimately more sales and more money. On the web, traffic is the new currency of power.

But as any seasoned insurance agent will tell you, the top dog agents far outperform the rest because they milk the most from their prospects by using smarter strategies. Similarly by attracting relevant traffic and using strong content you can achieve better conversion ratios than your competitors.

Whatever the mix of online marketing channels you use to generate traffic, your success rests on five key factors explained below.

Focus on Your Target Audience

Define your target audience. This may seem obvious but you need to think hard about your potential customers and their buying habits. You need to wear the buyer persona and define your target demographics.

What do they buy? What factors affect their buying decisions? How do they arrive at making a purchase decision? What are their preferred ways to search for the products they need? How can you increase their purchase intent? How frequently do they buy the product?

Smart marketers first understand their buyers. Based on the resulting analysis, they identify the best possible approaches to promote their products and services. Pitching your product to someone who does not need it or is not inclined to buy it can only be a drain on your resources.

Defining your target audience is important because it lets you identify the keywords that need to be used in SEO and PPC campaigns. It is also necessary to devise your content strategy for social media promotion. You need to know what your customers want to know so that you can write about it.

A deep perception of all the stages of buyer's decision-making cycle lets you target them with appropriate forms of content that are tailor made to the situation. For example, the way you write a marketing message to a prospective lead is significantly different from a past customer. The two situations need different styles of pitching.

Finally, understanding your audience helps you direct your entire online marketing effort to attract the relevant traffic. Focusing on relevant traffic produces higher conversion rates and increased returns on the investment.

Court Attention at All Cost

The proverbial wisdom of online marketing tells us that it takes about seven exposures to make your prospect remember your message. You need to capture their attention time and again on a regular basis.

You need to be everywhere on that particular portion of cyberspace your prospects go when searching, learning, using and buying the products and services you offer. Top the keyword searches. Hog the limelight with press releases, blog entries and social networks. Dominate your local business results and natural search results.

Work on promoting yourself as *the* expert in your field. When you achieve authenticity and credibility, your words elicit trust and you will be able to sell without trying too hard. But you need to work hard to become the all-knowing expert people would come to to know about things.

The Best Things on the Web are Free

So use them. Blogs, microblogs, video hosting sites, social networking sites, social bookmarking sites and article syndication cost nothing. Creating a smart viral campaign often produces better business results down the line than a poorly-conceived PPC marketing campaign.

Working meticulously on creating rich content and engaging positively to create a long term advantage may not seem as cool as indulging in more exciting pay per click and SEO campaigns but it usually produces long lasting results.

Understand that people want authenticity, not spin. On the web, marketing is a lot more than advertising. The people thronging social networking sites want participation, not propaganda. So focus on using the free online platforms to build your expert status just as much as you do on advertising.

Make a Nice Plan and Stick to It

Most online marketing strategies require sustained effort but produce cumulative result. You need to create a schedule for your campaign and stick to it. Consistency in delivering quality content is the key to build online reputation.

Posting an article and then disappearing for months will not produce results. People are information-hungry and need newer stuff to consume. Keep on posting the latest happenings in your market segment and develop long term relationship with them. But remember that quality outweighs quantity.

Track Everything

Online marketing offers wonderful tools to track and analyse even the minute details of a campaign. Use them to track your money, results and the effectiveness of the campaign. But beware not to fall too much in love with the metrics and statistics.

Set measurable goals and identify the key performance indicators for all the aspects of your campaign. By benchmarking yourself with the industry best, you can identify the marketing channels that are irrelevant and ineffective. That way you can delete them from your marketing mix and focus on the channels that produce optimum results with attractive ROI.

Capturing leads

When visitors express interest in your product or service they become leads. They may or may not actually end up buying your offering but they have expressed interest and that may lead to a purchase decision. Your job is to take their contact details to provide them with further information that may motivate them to make a buy decision.

Nothing can be more disappointing than to see hundreds of visitors log on to your web site and leave it without making a sale. You need a lead capturing strategy to identify and capture leads to progress one more step toward making a sale.

On an average, a mere 3% of visitors make a sale. A lot of small business owners focus too much and fret over that 3% and ignore the rest. A smart marketer understands that a significant proportion of that 97% will come back some time in the future and form a lion's share of revenue. So you need to have a mechanism to get their details and capture those leads.

Here is what you need to do –

1. First things first. A small proportion of visitors will always be fired up and ready to buy your product. You need to make it easy for them to make the transaction. Don't make them search all over the site to find out where to click to enter credit card information. Your site should be easy to navigate and be not more than two clicks away from receiving a financial payment.
2. Not all people who land up on your web page come from the same place and have the same intention. To pitch your services according to the level of purchase intent they have, you need to create different landing pages. For example, someone who came to your site via a PPC advertisement will be more inclined to buy your product than the one arriving through a search result. Also create a mobile web site for people accessing your site via mobile interface.
3. Landing page optimisation is a discipline in itself with a wide variety of techniques. Depending on the sets of keywords you have selected for your PPC campaign, you can design more than one landing pages to test which keywords work better in attracting traffic.
4. The simplest way to capture leads is to use a sign-up form asking for name, email address and perhaps mobile number of the visitor. The best results are usually obtained by using either a sidebar signup or pop-over rather than pop-up or pop-under forms.

We worked with Joe, the owner of a small kitchen design, manufacture and fitting company. He used to run what we call advertise and pray type campaigns. He would take out adverts in newspapers and run radio adverts telling people about the existence of his business.

This advertising would convert a small percent of people who would come to his showroom and look at his kitchens. Of these an even smaller percent would be ready to buy a kitchen then and there and he would do business with them.

We showed Joe how extremely wasteful this was. What about all the people who came to his showroom, liked his kitchens, but for some reason or another were not ready to buy? This is a classic case of focusing on 3% while ignoring the 97%.

We showed Joe how to capture the details of these prospects and capture the leads. Then we wrote twelve mailing pieces for Joe to keep in touch with his leads that included testimonials, case studies and facts about what makes his kitchen company different.

We then scheduled these articles to be sent once every month and took care of the fulfilment of this for him. Now there's a good chance the first few times Joe's prospects receive his information it will go straight to their wastebaskets. But after 5, 6, 7, 8 times they will start to notice.

And when they are ready to purchase a kitchen, who do you think is going to be their first point of contact?

The person they have never heard of in the Golden pages or Joe? The answer is obvious.

5. As people do not like to give their email address or phone number you must give them a reason to. Offer something free to download such as a free eBook or special report or

white paper containing useful information that soft-sells your business. Special discounts and free trial memberships also produce good results.

6. You need to effectively manage, sort and segment the contacts of your leads as the information will be used for future marketing campaigns and communication. There are many software applications that make this job easier for you. As soon as a visitor signs up on your web site the application activates auto-responder and sends an email acknowledging and thanking the registration.

7. The leads provide a huge opportunity to build a customer base and achieve repeat sales. Double opt-in leads (visitors who clicked on a confirmation email sent by you to complete the registration process) are of particularly high value.

Following up your customers with rich content

The leads have expressed an interest in your product but they really have not yet made up their minds on buying it. Now is the time to educate them about your product or service to heighten their purchase intent.

- Know your customer. Newsletters, email remainders, marketing brochures or white papers – no matter what the format of your marketing message, it has to convince the leads that buying your product is in their interests. To do that you need to have a deep understanding of the buyer's persona and buyer decision-making cycle. Understanding your buyers is a necessary ingredient of any effective content strategy.

- Someone who approached your web site via a PPC campaign may have a more immediate need and intent to buy your product. On the other hand, a visitor who lands up on your site through a search engine might just be looking for information with no inclination to order the service. They are at two different stages of buyer decision-making process and the way you appeal to them through your marketing message needs to take this fact into consideration.

One of our clients, Sue, wanted to start an alternative health business but wasn't sure how to go about finding leads and converting them into paying customers.

We created a search engine pay per click campaign driving traffic to a specially created web page that we set up for her. This page offered a Free Booklet on Stress Management that prospects could download in exchange for submitting their contact details.

We wrote a series of follow up emails offering further information and offering a complimentary session. These emails were then sent out to each prospect every week for 2 months. In addition we created a sequence of 12 postcards that we automatically send out on Sue's behalf to every prospect on her list each month.

These methods alone have given Sue a thriving business in less than 6 months. She is free to concentrate on what she does best, providing alternative health therapies, while we keep her marketing campaign running like clockwork giving her a steady supply of new business.

In fact Sue is so happy with what we have done for her in lead generation and conversion that we are currently setting up a customer retention system for her. This will include us creating and mailing a newsletter to each of her clients every month.

- Not all your prospects or leads have the same need and same approach to your product. In such a scenario, instead of designing one slick message that caters to all the potential customers, it is more effective to create different marketing messages targeting niche audiences with tailored content.
- Know your goals in designing marketing content. Do you want to educate your customer about the product? Or do you want to directly pitch the product with discounts or

its unique features? Or is it the time for a demo? How can you target your content to their specific industry, their job functions and the goals of their companies and to their geographic locales?

- Know your product. What is your USP? How different and appealing is it from other substitute products? What benefits does it bestow on your customers? Does it come with a warranty or money-back guarantee?
- Follow up your leads. Not all leads can be turned into customers within a single marketing campaign but you need to keep cultivating leads. You need to keep on working to create an image in their minds that you are the authority in your field. When the need to buy your service arises you should be the first person they remember and contact.
- Keep track of things. Regularly analyse the effectiveness of your marketing strategies and messages. This gives you an opportunity to find out what is working and what is not. You need to keep on tweaking your strategies to get the best out of them.

Gaining your prospect's confidence to make the sale

Making your lead make the sale can be tricky but not difficult. There are no short cuts and simple tactics here to achieve high conversion ratios. The key is to think long term and work on improving credibility and becoming an authority in your field.

As discussed before, online marketing is a bit different from offline marketing in the sense that it demands more authenticity and less spin. People place more trust in the suggestion of a friend than a salesperson. So instead of trying to hard-sell your product, it is more effective to seem like an expert suggesting a particular product.

This, of course, does not mean you should stop hard selling. Whatever the tone of the message it is more likely to produce the intended result when you and your site have authenticity.

With online fraud on the rise, scammers are making life difficult for honest people. To gain your customers' trust you need to humanise your web site. Live chats have been found to be helpful in making visitors feel more secure. The idea that someone is out there who is ready to answer their questions makes them feel at ease.

Make sure that your payment system is secure. Using third party verification seals and well-known payment gateways such as Visa, MasterCard and PayPal are likely to gain your prospect's trust to make the sale. Adopt easily navigable shopping cart programs to make the shopping experience more fun for your customers.

Chapter 3
Content-Driven Traffic Generation

Traffic is the life blood of any online marketing campaign. While search engine optimisation and PPC campaigns do well in generating traffic, adapting a content-driven strategy that aims to provide useful and informative content to your customers is more effective. By creating content that establishes you as a 'thought leader' in your market, you can make your customers come back to your site. By designing messages that people want to hear, you not only generate traffic but are also better placed to achieve your marketing goals.

What is content-driven traffic generation?

Without visitors we have nothing. All that effort you have put into designing an attractive web site is practically useless if nobody sees it. You need traffic. Generating traffic is the bedrock of any online marketing campaign.

PPC campaigns and other ad-based campaigns do generate quick traffic but the traffic volume quickly fades out as soon as you stop advertising. The traffic generated using such methods is generally not sustainable in the long term. Spending huge amounts on keyword bidding in PPC is not advisable either.

A content-driven traffic generation strategy relies on attracting visitors by regularly providing them with useful and interesting information that makes them revisit the site again and again.

Instead of relying on ads, offers and discounts to attract visitors, a content-driven strategy aims to position you as an authority of information in your market segment. You create the impression that you are the expert to listen to; that you have ideas that help people solve problems and that you are the person they can turn to for advise and do business with.

By establishing yourself as the 'thought leader' in your market you not only generate more traffic but can achieve high conversion ratios. The increased authenticity and credibility you create in the cyberspace further help you to up-sell and cross-sell more products and services to your customer base.

To generate traffic you need to be able to create interest in the minds of the people by capturing their attention with irresistible messages. The messages also need to be crafted to attract only the relevant traffic that has more inclination to buy your products and services.

These messages must be distributed via various web channels. Using a host of social media channels you need to create connections, build nodes and spread your messages. You cannot rely on only one message or only one avenue of delivery. You need to design different messages to different categories of customers and use an appropriate online delivery mix to get your message across.

Writing messages that people want to hear

You need to understand your customers to write content that engages them. How do you do that? One useful strategy that marketers often use is to create a buyer persona. A buyer persona is an archetype of your customers or a group of customers. It is a detailed profile that best captures your customers.

The buyer persona is not a description of the person or the profession he or she is in. It is a short biographical sketch that tries to capture the customer's background, daily routine, buying habits and the problems he or she faces.

To get the best results you need to ask some hard questions and come up with incisive answers. What are the goals and aspirations of your target audience? What problems do they face? What media and marketing channels do they use to find answers? How can you reach them? What words do they use while searching for information?

Depending on the nature of your business you might even create more than one persona profile to describe different groups of customers.

Here are two simple examples of buyer personas for a fast food restaurant business –

Businessman Ronald comes in almost every day at lunch time. He always wears a suit and drives an expensive car. High prices do not seem to affect him but he demands fast service. He always seems to be in hurry and becomes restless when items are not delivered in time.

Angela is a 40-year old mother with four children. She visits the restaurant at most once in a week. She usually ordered special items that were on promotion sale. She is very price-sensitive and first to complain when prices were revised upwards.

The buyer persona helps us to visualise the target audience and devise better marketing messages and strategies. In the above scenario, the two customers Ronald and Angela have different needs, expectations and buying habits.

A marketing message that stresses discount sales and low prices is more likely to strike a chord with Angela while the one that promotes fast service will appeal to Ronald. A buyer persona helps you write the message in the language your audience best understand.

Instead of imagining what people want from your business a better way is to go and ask them. Talk to people to get more information. You never know what insights those conversations may provide you.

How to write great web content

Whether you are writing for SEO or an online video, you need to ask these three questions –

1. Who is my audience?
2. What actions do I want them to take after reading?
3. What information do I need to provide to make them feel confident to take that action?

If your content has reasonable answers to these questions, then you have come up with effective content. Here are more guidelines that help you in writing great content.

- **Make it easy to read.** Use clear and concise headings that include the relevant keywords. Use headlines that give a glimpse of what the readers can expect from the article. Keep your paragraphs short. Use bulleted and numbered lists often. Include descriptive links wherever possible in the article.
- **Make it easy to follow.** Start your article with a summary or a lead that clearly tells what the article is all about. State your main point and explain the key points. Then supply other less important details.

- **Write for your audience, not your ego.** Avoid trying to make the product or the service appear more complex than necessary. Avoid trying to make yourself appear smarter than your readers. Use as much simple language as possible.
- **Tell people what to do.** Do not assume that your readers will do what you want them to do after reading the copy. You need to tell them with a call to action. Call-to-action sentences explicitly tell the readers what to do. They often work on the minds of the readers at subconscious level and entice them to take the desired action. Click here, Join now, Sign up, Get access, Call now, Download now, Send an email now, etc., are some examples.

Designing traffic generation strategy

People can reach your site through any of the following means –

- By typing the URL of your site in the browser's address bar
- Clicking on a result from the search engine results page
- Clicking on an ad or a link on the other site which leads to your web pages
- Through social networking and other social media means

The proportion of visitors approaching your site by these means can vary from business to business. Some small businesses depend largely on PPC campaigns and affiliate marketing. On the other hand, some businesses might be able to generate content that has 'sociability'. From a marketing point of view, you need to analyse the specific situation pertaining to your business and create a traffic generation strategy that intends to spend relevant amounts of money on these channels.

Generating traffic through SEO

People are more likely to click on organic results than paid results as they elicit more trust. This is the reason why no marketer can ignore search engine optimisation. Studies also show that 62 percent click on any of the top ten results. 90 percent do not go beyond the first three search engine results pages. 82 percent of people will change their keywords to get better results but do not migrate to other search engines[1].

When stripped of jargon-filled buzzwords and excessive neologism, the practice of SEO and its success is based on the following four factors –

1. Keywords
2. Content
3. Tags & URL paths
4. Inbound links

Why keywords are important

Your SEO campaign is only as good as your keywords. The success and failure of your search engine optimisation efforts depend heavily on the keywords you choose to optimise the campaign.

Every business has certain keywords to describe its products and services. These are the words that are most likely to be used by your potential customers to find you on the internet. In most cases, they are likely to be phrases or strings of keywords rather than single words. Identifying such keywords is the key to success of your SEO campaign.

How to find your magic keywords

Keywords are the essence of your business. Using keywords that are too generic or irrelevant and keywords that have low conversion can negatively affect the ROI of your campaign. Here are few suggestions that can help you in identifying your magic keywords -

- A simple way to spot the keywords that are relevant to your business is to look at what your competitors are using in their web sites. Check out the web pages of your

[1] iProspect, "iProspect Search Engine User Behavior Study," April 2006 (www.iprospect.com/premiumPDFs/WhitePaper_2006_SearchEngineUserBehavior .pdf)

competitors, specifically the industry leaders, which rank high and note down the keywords. You can view the source code of those web pages, go through the meta statements and find out the keywords to which those pages have been optimised.

- Check out the media sources that report on your industry. Industry associations, blog posts of industry experts, press releases of industry leaders, media reports and analysts can provide you with a glimpse into the keywords used by business, as well as the public, to interpret what is happening in the business.

- Use keyword research tools. There are many free and premium tools available online that help you in searching, identifying and filtering keyword lists. Wordtracker is a very popular keyword research tool on the web. (https://freekeywords.wordtracker.com/)
  Here is a list of more keyword research tools you can use –

  http://www.google.com/insights/search
  http://www.keyworddiscovery.com/search.html
  http://www.selfseo.com/keyword_suggestion_tool.php
  http://adlab.microsoft.com/keyword-Research.aspx

- SEO marketers classify keywords into three categories or three levels –

  Level 1 - Long, low-traffic descriptions. These are the phrases that are too long and try to describe the query as specifically as possible. They have low traffic but are easy to optimise for.
  Ex: 'catalytic converter recycling in county Meath Ireland'

  Level 2 - Medium, competitive strings. These are strings of two to five words that generally describe the nature of the product and service the user is looking for. These strings generate more leads and have good conversion rates. These are the words your SEO campaign needs to focus on.
  Ex: 'catalytic converters recycling in Ireland'

  Level 3 – Short, hyper-competitive keywords. These are short strings of keywords that generate the largest volume of traffic but resist the temptation to blow a fortune trying to optimise your site for these single- or two-word keyword phrases. Due to the intense competition as well as comparatively low conversion, small businesses should generally avoid them and instead focus on level 2 keywords.

Ex: 'catalytic converters' or 'catalytic converter recycling'.

How write copy for SEO

The fundamentals of writing engaging copy are the same everywhere but here are a few things you need to keep in mind while writing SEO copy.

- Use attention-grabbing headlines. 'How to hire and keep your best employees' is better than 'Creating an effective employee retention strategy'. The former title gives more information and helps the reader in making a better decision whether to continue to read the article or not.
- The most important thing in writing SEO copy is keywords. Once you have zeroed-in on your final list of keywords, you need to use them in your copy in an effective manner.
- The copy should at least be 250 words with chunked paragraphs. If the copy is longer than 800 words then consider splitting it into multiple web pages.

Get your tags and URL paths right

- The page URL, page title, meta description, meta keywords, headings and sub-headings should preferably have the keywords to which you wish the web page to be optimised. But take care that you don't stuff in too many.
- Instead of wasting the first few words to include the name of your business, use the most important keywords in the title and then follow them with your business name. For example, 'Staffing jobs in Ireland – careerjet.ie' is better optimised than 'Careerjet.ie – Staffing jobs in Ireland'.

- Build keywords into URL paths. The URL should describe the content of the page. 'www.yourdomain.com/how-to-choose-your-recycling-partner.html' is better optimised than 'www.yourdomain.com/articles/1.html'.
- Include links to your optimised web pages. If you are writing articles for syndication purposes, then you should consider including the phrases and keywords that describe your product and provide links to your optimised page.
- Include 'alt' tags (a short description that provides information about an image or video) to any images and videos you have used.

How to get more inbound links

The number of inbound links and the quality of those links is a very important determinant of your rank on the search engine results page. Here is what to do to get more link juice –

- Web pages featuring business product information or other mundane details such as 'about us' and 'what we do' have low 'bookmark-ability' and are not likely to get links from online community. Link exchange, PPC, affiliate marketing, link trading and directory listing are the only ways to get in-bound links to such pages.
- But by creating 'authority stuff' content, you can get more links with no additional expense. Building '101 lists', guides, informative articles such as '5 steps to (insert your topic)' and '10 ways to (insert your topic)', news & article syndication, white papers, special reports, eBooks and other downloadable stuff act as an online resource and get bookmarked by web users bringing inbound links.
- Avoid spamming blogs with links posted as comments. But links from blogs, especially those with high search engine ranking, are very helpful in boosting your page rank.
- Article syndication is a particularly useful tool as you can get 20 to 30 links just from one article. Press releases that have been intelligently written with optimised content are

also helpful in attracting link juice. You can even optimise press releases with keywords.

- Research indicates that spreading inbound links to both your home page as well as landing page by approximately 20-80 proportion produces best results[1].

- Focus on the quality of inbound links rather than quantity. Try to get as many links as possible from sites with high page rank.

Making your SEO more effective

- SEO is not a one-time exercise. It needs careful strategising, continuous refinement and rigorous execution to get the best results. You need to have patience to learn and experiment. There are many online resources that can help you master the art of search engine optimisation.

  http://www.seobook.com
  http://www.seomoz.com
  http://searchengineland.com
  http://www.searchenginejournal.com
  http://searchenginewatch.com
  http://www.seochat.com

- If you are in no position to take care of your SEO efforts or happen to lose your interest half-way, then it's time to hire a professional SEO firm to manage your online marketing campaigns. SEO is an ever-evolving field and it can be hard to follow-up with all the latest developments. Independent research indicates that SEO efforts by agencies produce nearly three times better results than in-house SEO campaigns[2].

- The ROI is more important than the process. Too often people fall in love with the excitement of new SEO techniques, tactics and processes and lose focus on the return on investment. Understand that the purpose of ROI is not just to get traffic but to make money. You need to work

---

[1] http://www.marketingexperiments.com/ppc-seo-optimization/how-to-improve-your-seo-clicks-and-conversions.html
[2] http://www.marketingexperiments.com/ppc-seo-optimization/how-to-improve-your-seo-clicks-and-conversions.html

on the content, on capturing leads and making an impression in the minds of the visitors.

- Regular review and analysis is a must. Devise key performance metrics such as the total number of visitors, average time spent on your site, number of pages viewed, number of leads, top search phrases, visitors from each search engine site and bounce rate, etc., to know how effective your campaign is. Using a host of tools and technologies, you can track pretty much everything about a SEO campaign. Here are a few popular SEO performance analysis applications –

    www.google.com/analytics
    www.haveamint.com
    www.webtrends.com
    http://web.analytics.yahoo.com

Generating traffic through forum posts

Forums or message boards are online sites where people can share their opinions in the form of posted messages. All the messages posted by different members are displayed in hierarchical structure. Users are free to start new discussions which are called threads and invite others to share their opinions.

There are two ways you can use forums to generate traffic to your site. One is to start a forum on your site and attract people to participate in its conversations. The other is to use forums and discussion boards relevant to your market segment and post messages with links that lead to your site.

To get more traffic through forums you need to find out what interests your target audience and then post topics that would attract them to come to your forums. You also need to keep in mind that not all subjects generate enough interest to make people participate in discussion forums.

When the topics posted in the forums are interesting people will naturally come back to check out what's happening. They bring their own opinions, traffic and of course, inbound links.

If you are posting your views on others' forums to attract traffic then you are advised to be subtle. Do not seem like a salesperson who is eager to sell his product but as a friend suggesting further information.

Some experienced forum marketers suggest using the signature effect in the control panel. With your links as your keyword optimised signature on your every post, people can easily click on the link and go to your web page.

Understand that forums related to your industry are more likely to attract relevant traffic as well as valuable inbound links. Make sure that your posts are in good taste and provide valuable information. Make your conversations interesting and traffic will follow.

Generating traffic through articles

Article marketing and syndication is a great way to promote your site. It not only gets you more links and traffic but also helps you establish yourself as an authority on the subject. Here are few guidelines that will help you write great articles –

- Write on what you know about the subject. If you do not know enough then do more research or hire professional writers. A few high quality articles that go viral will do the job of a hundred articles that strive to get noticed. Quality beats quantity.
- Monitor the web for new themes to write articles on. Keep watching industry news, organisations related to your market and your competitors to find out what's hot in the market.
- Write attention-grabbing titles. Use questions (How to lose weight in three simple steps?) and lists (5 ways to open wine without a corkscrew) in the titles of your articles to make them more interesting and also to tell the audience what to expect from the article.
- Identify the keywords you need to optimise your article for and use them in the title. There is no common consensus on the right keyword density for the article body.

Some people stuff too many keywords and make the article repetitive. Just remember that you need to optimise the article for humans rather than search engines.

- People who post their articles to the article directories are required to write a small 'about the author' description at the end of the article. Here you can write a beautiful introduction establishing yourself as an expert and include the URL of your website.

- There are many article directories on the web but the most popular among them are –

  www.ezinearticles.crom
  www.articledirectorry.com
  www.articlegold.com
  www.articlerich.com
  www.authorpalace.com
  www.articlesbase.com
  www.ehow.com
  http://aswann.net
  www.postarticles.com
  www.uberarticles.com
  www.articledashboard.com
  www.newarticlesonline.com

- Always publish the article on your website or blog first and then submit it to article directories. You need to wait for two or three days for the article to be indexed by the search engines before you begin sending them to article syndication sites.

Generating traffic through comments

Leaving comments on blogs with a link back to your own site is another way of attracting traffic. The earlier you make the comment the better it gets for your traffic. This is because most bloggers use RSS feeds that send the details of the new blog post to their subscribers. A large proportion of initial traffic to the blog will be from these subscribers and you can 'ride the wave'.

- Identify the best bloggers related to your market segment. The online popularity of the incoming link to your site adds more weight to your own page rank. So keep track of all the best blogs.

- Not all bloggers allow comments. Some allow comments but not links. But you need to hunt and find 'do-follow' bloggers who allow both comments and linking.

- Do not spam the blogs. Do not post advertisements. Nothing irritates bloggers more than being lowered to advertisement platforms. Post comments that tell a thing or two about what you think.

- Try to use the same keywords as you have optimised for your site in the comments. Avoid linking to the home page of your site. Link it to the article you have written on a similar topic. This makes your comment as a helpful addition rather than blatant self-promotion.

- Make it a routine to leave at least 5 to 10 comments every week on blogs related to your industry. Such consistency can produce a steady stream of traffic to your site.

Using social networks to generate traffic

Notwithstanding the buzz surrounding social media, the huge potential of social media is still underused when it comes to using it to generate traffic. The most important means to utilise social networks is to keep posting new articles on your site or blog and then submitting these links to various social networking sites.

Social networks can help you make people aware of your website and blog across the world. You can expect a huge amount of targeted traffic in a short duration of time.

In a marketing experiment[1], a blogger was hired at $10 per hour to create content and spread it over social networks for 12 months. Then a 30-day test of Google AdWords PPC campaign was conducted bidding up to 75 cents per keyword.

Social media optimisation yielded 93,207 visitors and the total expenses were $3,600 with a cost per visit at 4 cents. On the other hand, the PPC campaign has been able to generate 2,057 visitors

[1] http://www.marketingexperiments.com/ppc-seo-optimization/social-media-optimized.html

with the total costs amounting to $1,250 at 61 cents per visit. The social media optimisation produced 1,427 percent more results than the PPC campaign.

- To get the best results on social networking sites, you need to focus on building connections, not on closing sales. Instead of being an online salesperson, you have to work on becoming a problem-solver and a resource person who can help others solve their problems. The resources you can provide can include not just articles but also product reviews, service comparisons, software downloads, white papers, special industry reports, surveys, podcasts, online videos, how-to guides, free services, opinion-based content such as blogs and advice.

- Attract new nodes, that is, new members but focus on people who network a lot. As the number of people you can reach via social networking and bookmarking sites increases, the traffic to your site too will be on a rise with a multiplying effect (Metcalfe's Law states that a network increases exponentially with the number of nodes).

- Identify effective social platforms on various sites to participate in conversations with your potential customers. Build a list of fan pages, discussions and groups whose members are likely to be your potential customers.

- As discussed earlier, you are more likely to be popular on social networks when you provide useful and informative content on a regular basis than when you try to hard-sell your products. Invest in the community and over the time you will reap the benefits.

- Quickly spread your articles on various social networks using smart online tools such as shareholic[1] and socialmarker[2]. Socialmarker allows you to upload links to your articles and web pages on about 50 social networks in just less than 15 minutes. Instead of trying to work on each network one by one you can promote a page across the social network space at once.

- Become your own customer. Keep posting comments and spread the links to your site posing as a customer (under

---

[1] www.shareholic.com
[2] www.socialmarker.com

a different identity, of course). Keep creating buzz around your products and services. If you do not have the time and patience to do it all then hire people to do it.

- Follow the happening events in your business to identify opportunities to write articles on and create buzz. If such events can be predicted (such as the next exhibition related to your industry) then prepare the necessary content beforehand and time it to the occasion to generate huge occasional traffic.
- Another way to use social networks to create traffic is to advertise in them. While this costs money, the results can be impressive depending on the nature of the products or service you are promoting. On social networks such as FaceBook and MySpace, people voluntarily reveal a lot of information which may provide insights into their buying habits and purchase intent. By advertising to such targeted audience, you can get more conversions.

Generating traffic through video content

With search engines fine-tuning their algorithms to provide better video search results, the practice of video SEO is continually evolving. With the kind of potential it has to generate traffic and interact with your audience, online videos are a must in your traffic generation strategy.

- Video SEO is more than posting video clips on YouTube. You need to optimise the videos to suit your marketing objectives. Since search engines cannot see what's inside the videos, you have to take care in optimising the data around the video.
- The title of the video should effectively describe the content of the video and also include the keywords. A lot of video experts suggest submitting the video content in the form of XML feed.
- The text you place around the video link on your page is perhaps the most important information taken into account by search engine algorithms while generating search results. You need to place the name of the video, the description of the video and the meta-tags related to

video in close proximity to the video clip on the web page.

- Always use thumbnails in your videos. When people search for videos in search engines, the clips with thumbnails stand out from those with dark screens.

- Create videos with your customers in focus. You don't need to blow a fortune preparing high-quality professional videos. Remember that you are making online videos, not television commercials. A simple conversation that connects with the audience at a more personal level will do the job very effectively.

- Apply the various social media optimisation techniques discussed in the previous sections to online videos as well. Videos are contagious and have more potential to go viral than articles.

Using podcasting to generate more traffic

Podcasting is digital radio or video programming that is downloadable from the internet. You can think of it as radio except that you can download and listen to it at your own convenience. iTunes (http://www.apple.com/itunes/) is by far the most popular podcasting platform (or podcatcher) though several others exist such as –

http://gpodder.org/
http://juicereceiver.sourceforge.net/
http://www.odeo.com/
http://www.podcast.com/
http://www.yasssu.com/
http://podceiver.com/
http://www.podnova.com/
http://silverfinn.net/podtower
http://pull.codeplex.com/

Software applications like QuickTime Pro and Apple's Garage Band let you create your own podcasts at home. They make recording, editing, mixing and formatting your podcasts very easy and ready for uploading.

Podcasting is relatively inexpensive but appeals only to a narrow band of audience. The content of the podcast needs to be of high quality with high information use-value without which it becomes difficult to maintain people's interest.

You need to be creative and come up with interesting ideas on what to podcast about. However, popular wisdom tells us that if a message is best delivered as an article – to be read – then it is best to keep it that way rather than trying to make it a podcast – to be listened to. Interviews, expert discussions and customer opinions are more suited for podcasting.

You can produce better results with a companion blog that discusses the contents of the podcasts. Another advantage is the text used in the blog gets indexed by the search engines and helps to get noticed.

Instead of looking at podcasts strictly as traffic generation tools, you need to think of it as a way to augment your other online marketing objectives. Podcasts are a wonderful way to bond with your audience, to inform and entertain them and to create more positive experience for your customers.

Chapter 4
Paid Traffic Generation

Paid traffic can do wonders for your business, especially if you are just starting out on the web. It is probably the quickest way to get traffic to your site but the effects last only as long as you are willing to pay for it. To make the most of any paid traffic campaign, you need to have a clear understanding of your target audience and the best keywords that help you get to them. An advantage of paid traffic is you can test offers rapidly to see how effective they are. With the kind of control paid traffic tools offer, you can quickly identify what appeals most to your audience.

What is paid traffic generation?

Paid traffic refers to any kind of traffic you get by paying for it such as pay per click advertising, banner ads or display advertising and affiliate marketing. The ads can be contextual (text-based), images, animations or location maps.

Paid marketing usually produces immediate results but the effects wear off faster once you stop marketing. The start-up costs are usually low for paid marketing but in the long term organic search marketing and social media optimization are more cost effective than paid marketing.

Another disadvantage of paid traffic generation is it elicits less trust than organic search results and social media marketing. However, paid marketing is a great tool to generate traffic if you are just starting up your website or launching a new product.

Some of the most important channels of paid traffic generation are –

1. Advertising in social networks such as FaceBook
2. Pay per click (PPC) advertising
3. Banner advertising
4. Affiliate marketing

How to use social networks such as FaceBook to generate traffic

Social networks such as FaceBook offer a superb marketing platform for businesses. People signing up for social networks usually reveal a lot of personal details and that helps marketers to target the users on a variety of parameters such as location, age, gender, language, profession, education and various personal interests. Marketing to such focused audiences produces highly effective campaigns.

FaceBook offers more than 500 million potential customers to do business with. Using simple image and text-based ads, you can promote your product or build a brand or form a community around your business.

FaceBook also offers high control over your budget spend just like Google AdWords. You can choose to opt for CPC (cost per click) method or CPM (cost per thousand impressions) and set your daily budget and overall campaign budget.

To get the best from FaceBook, follow these smart online marketing tactics –

- Define your target audience. FaceBook[1] lets you identify your potential customers by age, gender, location and their personal interests. If you are a local business then you can target your audience by location.
- You can add either a target URL in your ad or redirect them to your (or your business') FaceBook page. People do not even have to visit your page. They can 'become a fan' or click on 'RSVP to this event' (RSVP - *répondez s'il vous plaît* which means 'reply please' or 'please respond') on the ad itself.
- Write an attention-grabbing headline (which is limited to 25 characters including spaces). Then you are left with another 135 characters to describe your message. So a lot of effort needs to be put into designing your FaceBook ads. Keep in mind that the image you add to the advertisement needs to be relevant and thought-provoking.
- Keep testing your ads. Sometimes changing the image to a more suitable one produces better results. Create multiple ad versions and run them to find out what works best. Keep on fine-tuning your ads using tools like FaceBook Insights[2].
- On your fan page, you can post white papers, special reports, links to informative articles, guides and webinars that help people. Try to engage them with useful content rather than hard-selling your products. That way, you get more leads and elicit greater trust.

---

[1] http://www.FaceBook.com/help/?page=863
[2] http://www.FaceBook.com/insights

Traditional marketing campaigns have a large element of waste, for example with direct mail some pieces will not be delivered or the people targeted will not have an interest in the product or service. When it costs 55c to get an item delivered this waste can quickly add up.

Using pay per click advertising can be much less wasteful as you will only pay for the clicks that you generate. There is still however a high degree of waste, albeit with minimal monetary cost, in terms of the amount of ads that need to be displayed to generate a click. Pay per click can be targeted by geographical location and tied to a search term which gives pretty good targeting, but it can be improved on even further.

FaceBook advertising and mobile advertising on smartphones allows even more targeting of adverts. For example, imagine if you were selling a speciality dog food and you had identified that 80% of your customers were women it would be possible to target adverts based on location, age, sex and interests.

You can choose to target women aged 18 or over within 10 miles of Dublin who like Dogs. This would give you a highly targeted list of a few thousand people. You could now test a number of different advertising approaches to get the attention of these people in a focused way.

The same can be done using smart phone advertising networks such as Admob. Want to do this for your own business? Just take the time to draw up a profile of your perfect customer. Then using that profile set up a filter on your FaceBook advertising account that best matches who you are targeting.

You can test it very easily without investing much money. Once you make it work then you can roll out similar campaigns for other customer profiles that would be interested in your products and services.

- Much like AdWords, FaceBook offers a multitude of control options on your budget spend. You can set daily budget limits or campaign limits with specific time limits. Research also suggests that the CPC model is slightly better than CPM model. Choose what suits your business best but remember not to overspend in the initial stages of marketing campaigns.

- Avoid creating multiple accounts on FaceBook. This is against the terms and conditions of FaceBook. Instead create only one FaceBook fan page and engage your audience from that page. Also do not spam users with your ads. It is counter-productive and sometimes may also invite a ban from FaceBook.

- FaceBook's fan page is almost like having a web site. You can offer content, add applications, include sign-up pages and promote events like discount sales. It is a great relationship building platform. FaceBook also allows you to create different tables, each with its own URL. These URLs can be used to promote different categories of the content you create.

Pay per click (PPC) marketing

Pay per click advertising is a model wherein the advertisers pay only when potential customers click on their adverts. Advertisers have to bid on keywords or keyword phrases that are relevant to their markets.

Google AdWords[1], Yahoo! Search Marketing[2] and Microsoft adCenter[3] are the three largest network operators on the web and pretty much cover all markets in the world. All these networks operate on bid-based models.

The advantage of PPC over other forms of advertising is that the adverts are displayed to the potential customers after they have expressed intent by typing the keywords on the search engine.

---

[1] http://www.google.com/adwords
[2] http://searchmarketing.yahoo.com/
[3] http://adcenter.microsoft.com/

It is easy for new marketers to get drawn into bidding wars for high-competition keywords. When coupled with poor PPC optimization, the results produced are often not worth the effort.

We understand that small businesses are short of cash. Trying to increase the number of leads or sales without increasing spending on PPC ads can be challenging but not impossible. Here we will explain some smart online marketing strategies and tactics to squeeze every ounce of profits from your PPC campaigns.

How to avoid keyword pricing trap

To get the best ROI from your PPC campaign –

- Avoid bidding wars to get high-competition keywords unless you have deep pockets.
- Increase keyword buys in the long-tail opportunities.
- Optimise post-click conversion rates by writing effective ad copy and designing an appealing landing page.
- Optimise your PPC ads to make them more effective.

The making of a smarter PPC campaign

Optimising a PPC advertising campaign needs practice, testing and a bit of tweaking. You need to use more than one advert in a campaign to identify the best one that does the job. Do not stop even after you achieve your intended results. Keep on fine-tuning various aspects of your advert and PPC campaign.

- Focus on identifying the most relevant keywords. They convert better and produce better ROI than other keywords and phrases that are not appropriate for your offer.
- If your desired keywords are too expensive then go for deeper keywords with more words in the phrase. Such more specific keyword phrases may produce less traffic but usually convert better and can be purchased for less money.
- When deciding the keyword groups, think broad rather than deep. 200 keywords at $0.15 perform better than 150 keywords at $0.50.

- Create customised landing pages for each specific key-word category. Since visitors come with different purchase intentions, the copy on the landing pages needs to fill different expectations.

- If the PPC visitors do not buy the product but sign-up by giving an email, then follow them with an effective email marketing strategy. Build a list of such opt-in email lists as they serve as a pool of potential customers you can target later.

- Write different copies of advert to test what works best. See how you can further enhance the effectiveness of the copy. While a good copy should produce a good click-through rate (number of clicks on the ads that lead to a landing page), you also need to keep an eye on the actual sales conversions on the landing page.

- If an advert is attracting a lot of clicks but poor conversions, then the copy is probably creating too much hype. There are two disadvantages of hype. First, it creates scepticism and deters visitors with strong purchase intent. And then, it attracts the wrong kind of visitors which leads to more clicks but poor conversions.

- Keep tracking the campaign. Identify the metrics that would help you track the effectiveness of the campaign. Key performance indicators such as clicks, average cost per click, PPC fees, number of orders, conversion rate, average order, total sales, net profit before PPC fees, net profit after PPC fees and return on investment are some important indicators you must use to analyse your campaign.

- Do not just stick to the big PPC advertising networks. There are many other smaller advertising platforms you can use. While the traffic may not be as high as the bigger networks, you get to enjoy lower keyword pricing and comparatively better click-through rates. Some networks you can consider using are –
  AdBrite (http://www.adbrite.com)
  Bidvertiser (http://www.bidvertiser.com)
  Clicksor (http://www.clicksor.com)
  Adonion (http://www.adonion.com)
  AdOptim (http://www.adoptim.com)

90 Degree Media (http://90degreemedia.com)
AdToll (http://www.adtoll.com)
Kontera (http://www.kontera.com)

- An important bidding strategy is to avoid using round increments (such as $0.10, $0.20, $0.30, $0.50) while bidding for keywords. Bidding one or two extra pennies often helps you secure significant boost in placements.
- Monitor your competition to see what they are doing. It can often produce wonderful insights into how they are approaching their PPC campaigns.
- Understand that PPC is ever-evolving. You need to test, analyse and optimise your campaigns to get the best results. Do not stop improvising even after you are satisfied with the results.

How to write great PPC adverts

The foremost purpose of an advert is to get the user click on the link to visit your website. Often the effectiveness of adverts is measured in the clicks they produce but the conversions they ultimately lead to is also a metric you should ponder.

PPC search engines allow multiple ad copies for the same ad group. This helps a lot in testing, analysing and optimising the ad copy. You can tweak the copy until it meets your requirements and produces the desired results.

- "If you have just 15 words to explain to people why they should buy from you, what would they be?" This question pretty much sums up the challenge involved in writing PPC adverts.
- You need to think deeply about the value proposition you are offering to your potential customers. For a value proposition to be appealing and effective, it needs to score highly on three parameters –
  1. Appeal – How desirable is your offer?
  2. Exclusivity – Why your offer is not available elsewhere?
  3. Credibility – How true are your claims about your offering?

- Understand that the value you promise to your visitors should outweigh the costs of the immediate action you wish them to take such as clicking on a link to your landing page. A good advert has a clearly identifiable value proposition while a bad advert has a poorly identifiable value proposition.

- Also understand that the value proposition you make in the PPC advert should be followed by a similar or better value proposition on the landing page. If there is a mismatch between them, then the conversions may suffer.

- Include your keywords in the ad copy. Whenever the keywords typed in the query by the user

Ads

Bedroom Wardrobes
Amazing Deals on Bedroom Wardrobes
Low Prices & Fast Irish Delivery
pinesolutions.co.uk

Wardrobes Online
Range of Stylish Wardrobes to suit
all tastes @ Littlewoods Ireland!
www.littlewoodsireland.ie

sliding **wardrobes** & doors
amazing value, made to measure
buy on line, delivered in ireland
www.robesdirect.ie

Wardrobes at Argos
A Wide Range of Wardrobes at Argos
Check, Reserve & Collect for Free!
www.argos.ie/Wardrobes

Cream French Furniture
Massive savings on hand-made French
-style furniture
www.solomonsoutlet.ie

Bedroom Furniture
Find A Great Deal On BuyandSell.ie
Search 1000s Of New & Used Products
www.buyandsell.ie

Bedroom Wardrobes?
Bedroom Wardrobes at low prices
Bedroom Wardrobes at Shopping.com
uk.shopping.com/Bedroom wardrobes

Figure 4.1 PPC Adverts

matches the keywords in the ad copy, they appear as bold. This increases the relevance as well as improving the quality score of your ad copy on the Google AdWords algorithm.

- Specificity converts. The more specific your keywords are the better your conversion rate will be. Differentiate yourself from your competition by using words that tell your USP. Note how various words such as 'stylish' and 'made to measure' were used in the ad copy to differentiate a business from the rest in the sample ads shown for the search phrase 'bedroom wardrobes'. You can also see how ads state their USPs such as 'low prices', 'fast delivery' and 'collect for free' in the ad copy.

- Include your most relevant keyword in the display URL used in the ad copy. This increases the quality score of the algorithm and also elicits greater trust. Notice how some ads use 'wardrobes' in the URL.

- Use quantitative statements over vague terms to state your proposition. For example, '1000s of used and new products' is much better than 'many products' or 'a range of products'.

- Include your most relevant keyword in the display URL used in the ad copy. This increases the quality score of the algorithm and also elicits greater trust. Notice how some ads use 'wardrobes' in the URL.

- Use quantitative statements over vague terms to state your proposition. For example, '1000s of used and new products' is much better than 'many products' or 'a range of products'.

- Set expectations but make sure that you deliver. One ad copy in the above example promises 'massive savings'. If the company is able to meet the expectation then it's good but if they can't it can be counterproductive.

- Can you offer the lowest price? Do you have the best quality products in your category? Do you offer high-quality premium products? What is your strongest selling point (Ex: Faster delivery, excellent customer service)? Do you offer any guarantees, warranties, bonuses, 30-day free trials? The answers can give you an idea of what expectations you can set in the ad copy.

- Try to create a sense of urgency in your ad copy by using phrases like 'limited offer' or 'available for overnight shipping' or 'offer while stocks last'.

- Use credibility indicators such as money-back guarantee, three year warranty and No.1 rated company. They elicit trust and increase the click-through rates as well as conversions.

- Keep testing your ad copies. The only way you can find out what works is to test, analyse and optimise the copies until you reach the best.

How to generate traffic with banner advertising

Banner advertising refers to small rectangular ads that we see on various web pages. They vary in size and content but, just like PPC advertising, they take you to the advertiser's website when we click on them.

Before the arrival of PPC advertising, banner advertising was the most popular means of internet marketing. But with more effective and more contextual nature of pay per click ads, banner advertisements have lost their sheen.

However, with the advent of appealing flash programming and graphic design software applications, banner advertising is attracting more marketers than ever. Here are a few tips you can use to get the best results from display advertising –

- Just like PPC advertising, you need to be able to define and identify your target audience. When your ad is placed in a website that has no relevance to your customer base, it cannot achieve its intended purpose.
- Check out the web to make a list of sites, blogs and forums that your potential customers frequently visit. Identify the ones with most traffic. Understand that unlike PPC, advertising in few sites that have high traffic often produces better results than advertising in a hundred sites that see less traffic.
- Make sure that your banner is creative and appealing to the eye. Hire professional flash animators and graphic designers to create rich media banner ads. Instead of in-your-face flashing ads that gives headache to people, go for ads that are high on aesthetics.
- Do not include audio and video that plays automatically. They are not only annoying but irritate visitors so much they would rather go away from the site than turn off the

sound. Always use play buttons and give your visitors some control over how the banner ad should play.

- Advertisers can bid on banner ads on CPM (cost per thousand impressions) or CPC (cost per click) or CPA (cost per action) basis. CPM refers to the number of people who actually viewed your ad irrespective of whether they clicked on it or not. CPC refers to number of visitors who clicked on the ad to arrive at the landing page. CPA refers to the number of people performing a specific action such as downloading a sample or adding an item to the shopping cart or making a sale.

- If you run a test ad for some time, then you will be better able to find out which model works out best to you. For example, if 1000 people view the ad but only 50 people click on it, out of whom only 5 people buy the product worth €100, then it means that the yield of the entire campaign is €500. So you can afford to spend €500 per one CPM or €10 per one click.

Paid traffic through affiliate marketing

Though overlooked, affiliate marketing is an effective pay-per-performance model that immensely helps small businesses, especially e-retailers. But it has its own set of challenges and you need to use some smart strategies to avoid various pitfalls that dot affiliate marketing. The five greatest challenges that any affiliate marketer should take care of are –

1. Finding and recruiting high quality affiliates
2. Retaining high quality affiliates
3. Monitoring affiliate fraud and taking corrective actions
4. Formulating optimal affiliate rules regarding search and email marketing
5. Monitoring the use of your trademarks and brands by your affiliates

Here is what you need to do make the most of affiliate marketing.

- Research shows that affiliate marketing contributes to nearly 12% of total revenues of the organizations but 51%

of those sales come from the top 10% of the affiliates. This highlights the importance of finding and recruiting high quality affiliates.

- Search through various affiliates networks. Observe the PPC ads on search engines to find out the sites that attract the traffic related to your potential customers. Tell them that you have some products that may interest their visitors and provide an attractive offer.

- To attract top affiliates you need to be generous with your margins. Many high performing affiliates depend solely on the income from their affiliate programs. Treat them as your strategic partners rather than sales agents. Be psychologically prepared to increase their commissions with their increasing contribution. Otherwise you will not be able to retain them for long.

- Understand that affiliate marketing campaigns take some time to build reputation and deliver impressive results. If you keep on investing the required time and effort the results will be mucsh better than many other forms of online marketing.

- Many key affiliates often create their own marketing campaigns for your products using their resources. Extend all possible cooperation in building customised landing pages as well as custom codes to track their marketing efforts.

- Let your affiliates link to the interior pages on your site. Forcing them to link only to the home page may get you some traffic but it affects the conversions.

- Discuss thoroughly with your affiliates how to use your trademarks, logos and other branded items. Both the merchant and the affiliates need to have a clear understanding about how to use copyrighted stuff in PPC advertising, email promotional letters and others.

- Track your affiliates all the time to identify the ones who outperform others. Sometimes, people who ordered through your affiliates may reorder directly from you. While this saves you some commission, you should perhaps think of some way to reward your affiliates to motivate them to continue promoting your products and services.

- Notify your affiliates of any special promotions, discounts, new product launches and other special deals beforehand. This gives them time to design new landing pages and other marketing communications stuff.
- Use multiple affiliate networks for your offers and keep tracking the performance of your offers to find out the best platforms. This helps you identify the top performers so that you can devote the required time and effort. Some of the best affiliate networks on the web include –

    Experience Advertising
    (http://experienceadvertising.com)
    NET Exponent LLC (www.netexponent.com)
    Affiliate Announcement
    (http://www.affiliate-announce.com/affiliate-announcement.aspx)
    AffiliateCrew (www.affiliatecrew.com)
    IMarketing Ltd. (www.imarketingltd.com)
    MediaTrust (www.mediatrust.com)
    MGECOM, Inc. (www.mgecom.com)
    Commission Junction (www.cj.com)
    Paulson Management Group
    (www.paulsonmanagementgroup.com)
    VastPlanet Corp (www.vastplanet.com)

- Interact with your key affiliates to identify more ways to promote the products and services. Share all the required information regarding the products and your views on the best way to market them.
- Always be available to your high performance affiliates. You should actually appoint a dedicated employee to take care of all communication with your top affiliates.

Chapter 5
Optimising Your Website

You have about six seconds to impress the visitors to your website. The first impression you create will not only set the expectations but also determine the number of leads and conversions you will have in the end in a very significant way. However, a website is not just about aesthetics. It needs to score high on content, usability, appearance, structure and navigability. By optimising your website to make it more shareable, more linkable and more SEO-friendly, you will be able to better bond with your visitors and convert a significant number of them into customers.

What makes a website well-structured?

There are four basic aspects of websites any designer should take care of. They are –

1. Content
2. Usability
3. Appearance
4. Structure

Content

People primarily use the web to find information. The design considerations of any website should revolve around how to present the content in the most user-friendly way instead of aesthetics. Some of the most popular websites on the net (think Google and Amazon) are known for their simplicity rather than flashy designs. Here are few things you need to keep in mind when presenting the content to your visitors.

- Make the content easily readable by using distinct and descriptive headlines. Use small paragraphs to chunk the information. Bulleted lists make it easier for readers to scan the content faster. Highlighting important words and phrases is also a good idea.

- Like the newspapers, present the most important part of the information at the top of the page. As you go downwards, you can present the more mundane details.

- Avoid using pop-ups, pop-unders, blinking images, flashing lights, audio and video files that start automatically, splash pages and resizing of the windows. They are very distracting.

- Analyse how much content you have to work with, how much of it is inter-related and what kind of navigational structure is best suited to present that information. Using mind maps and hierarchical diagrams helps you visualise the structure of the content.

- Use interlinking profusely when presenting related information. If there is another web page on your site with similar or related information, then you should provide the links instead of waiting for the readers to poke around to find more.

- At the end of the day, your content should reflect the value proposition your organisation wants to make. Any narratives you use should be simple and relevant to the claims your value makes.

Usability

The usability aspect of the website refers to user-friendly nature, interface and navigability. Simply put, don't make your users figure out where to look and what to do next. They should just be able to do it with minimal effort.

- Stick to standard conventions. There is no point in being different for the sake of being different. As the web evolved certain standards have set in such as logo in the top left, menu options at top or left and links in blue colour. It makes various elements of the website easy to find.
- If your site has more than 10 pages then you should perhaps seriously consider using sitemaps. It is better to use dynamic sitemaps that are automatically updated as soon as a new web page is added.
- The information should be structured with the customer in mind. The topics should flow from broad to narrower categories. The content should be categorised appropriately.
- Navigation should guide the users easily from top-level pages to deeper web pages. The logo on the top left should always be linked to the home page. You should make it easy for users to know where they are in the site.
- Use global navigation, that is, a perpetual menu that appears on every page on the header just below the logo graphic. This lets visitors jump from one page to another without having to go back.
- Always enable the 'back' button. It is the most used tool when navigating web pages. Websites that use flash for the entire site are at a disadvantage.

- Unless absolutely necessary, such as displaying 'help' tips, do not open new browser windows when a link is clicked, even for external links.
- Avoid using obtuse visual icons in menus such as an image of wrench for options. Most users find them confusing and it spoils their web surfing experience.
- If you are using drop-down menus then make sure that they adhere to the web standards of HTML and CSS. Always offer a large hit area on the menu to make it easy for mouse movements.
- Use breadcrumb links on the top. They leave a trail of the links and represent the directory path. It helps visitors to know where they are and also to go back to where they were previously.
- Test your website in all popular browsers, including text-only browsers. If mobile marketing is an important part of your marketing mix, then perhaps you should seriously consider setting up a mobile-version of the website for users accessing the site through mobile browsers.
- Make your site accessible to people with disabilities. Let them be able to change the text size easily. Tag your images with relevant descriptions for people who use screen-reading software applications.
- Use a search box. Do not underestimate the people who use this function. If your search algorithms are bad, then use Google's in-site search option.

Appearance

People always trust their first impressions, even if they are naive. Making your website attractive is not about indulging in multimedia creativity but making it very easy for your visitors to access the information and guiding them subtly to perform the desired actions.

- The site should be easily scannable. It shouldn't take long to get an idea of how the site is organised and what its meaning is.
- Organise the site from the user's perspective as well as marketing perspective. The ultimate goal of any website is

to convert traffic into customers. So the way your site facilitates the sales funnel is very important.

- Lead capture should be given utmost importance. Use slide menus to capture leads. Or assign prominent space on the home page to collect the information of visitors.

- Avoid cluttering your web pages. There should be enough white space to make it easier to understand what is what. Avoid unnecessary animations as they drain the bandwidth and serve no marketing purpose.

- Use different colours to present different kinds of information. Checked and unchecked links should be easily distinguishable. Use lines, bars and dashes of various colours to separate different chunks of content.

- The graphics and text should follow the same style throughout the site. The consistency of the visual appearance is an important factor that affects the perception of your website at a subconscious level.

- Images communicate value with greater force and the copy with greater precision. You need to get the right balance between them. Experiments reveal that a right composition can increase your conversions by 29%[1].

- Avoid using stock images that have no or little relevance. Use only those images that have a direct implication for the value of your products and services.

- Choose the proportion of images carefully. Too much weight of an image can eclipse other elements of the page such as content. There are five aspects of images that affect their perception and you must manage them justifiably –
  1. Size
  2. Shape
  3. Colour
  4. Position
  5. Motion across the web page

- The copy of a web page should provide specific information and use the right tone. Try to use quantitatively specific statements over qualitative statements when propos-

---

[1] http://www.marketingexperiments.com/improving-website-conversion/images-vs-copy.html

ing your value. For example, "*We use the most accurate sampling procedures to estimate the recyclables in your scrap*" makes a qualitative statement. On the other hand, the statement "*Our sampling procedures accurately determine the recyclables in your scrap to a precision of 99.89%*" uses quantitative numbers and makes a better impression in the minds of the readers.

- The tone of your copy should be active and filled with call-to-action phrases. Avoid using passive sentences and academic tone. Do not use hyperbole. Overpromising and under-delivering can be very counterproductive in the long run.

- Eye tracking studies on reading patterns of web users tell us that people follow an F-pattern while viewing a web page. Their concentration is densest at the upper left corner, a long tail down the left side and two horizontal sides to the right. And the least activity is at the bottom right hand corner of the page. No wonder why smart website designers use a global navigation panel on the top of the page.

- Eye tracking studies also reveal that people usually ignore overdesigned graphics, images and flash animations. They are almost synonymous with advertisements and users divert their attention away from them almost unconsciously. Relying too much on flash animations to propose your value may not yield the desired results.

Structure

The structure of the website should focus on conveying your unique value proposition to visitors in a user-friendly as well as a search engine-friendly manner. To be able to do that, you need to know what your content is, how best to present it and the structure that supports such objectives.

- The information architecture of the site should carefully interlink the web pages and make the entire site readable by the search engine crawlers. Include a robots.txt file to make indexing easier.

- Avoid duplicates such as –
  http://mywebsite.com,
  http://www.mywebsite.com and
  http://www.mywebsite.com/index.html,
  as it dilutes the page rank. Use re-directs to point the traffic to a single version.

- Keep the file size of each web page as small as possible to enable faster downloads. The rule-of-the-thumb size limit for a web page is 150 KB.

- The purpose of a site is to get traffic, to capture as many leads as possible and convince many of them to make a purchase decision. The structure of the site should facilitate these transformations in a fluid manner.

- To gain credibility in the minds of the visitors, use third party logos and links. Also display logos of prominent associations and industry bodies you are part of and any awards you have won.

- Always include an informative 'about us' page. People still prefer to do business with real people with real offices. Include office address, phone numbers, fax numbers and email addresses of your important staff.

- Check your content for spelling and grammatical mistakes. While not many visitors will be sensitive to the errors, their presence makes your site look unprofessional.

- There are many standard layout languages used in web designing such as HTML (HyperText Markup Language), XML (eXtensible Markup Language), XHTML (eXtensible Hypertext Markup Language), CSS (Cascading Style Sheets), DOM (Document Object Model), the most popular one being CSS. As far as possible, use CSS. It reduces page loading times and bandwidth. It is also easier to maintain and update sites built on CSS.

- Use URL paths that describe the directory paths in a clear and unambiguous manner. For example, a URL with the path –
  www.domain.com/index.html?dir=domain&action=product &id=145 is less SEO-friendly than say
  www.domain.com/products/automotive-components/tank-units3.htm.

- When writing alt tags for images, use a description that is relevant to the context in which the image is being used. Titles like image1.jpg or topimage.jpg serve no SEO purpose as search engines cannot read the images, but only the tags associated with the images.
- Use clear and concise title tags to all web pages. Understand that the title tag is what is displayed when your web page is bookmarked or displayed in the search engine results page.
- Fill your meta tags of the web pages with an appropriate description of the content inside them. With SEO marketers abusing meta tags with excessive number of keywords, search engines no longer count the keywords in the tags when calculating page rank but the description is still displayed in the search results under the page title. This helps the visitor to have a glimpse of what the page contains.
- Check the site for any broken links. Avoid leaving 'under construction' pages. That leaves your site in a poor light. If you are not finished with any web page, don't show it. Activate web pages only after they are complete and working.

Optimising Your Site Using CMS

CMS or Content Management Systems allow you to control the entire content of the site – text, images, links, ads, videos and more – from a single application. These applications run on servers and the content of the websites are tied to them.

Using a CMS you can easily add, edit, delete and update content and even change the template of the website from any location in the world. There are literally hundreds of CMS applications available on the net and some of them are free and opensource.

When choosing a CMS for your website keep in mind that –

- The selected CMS should be easily able to manage the content as it scales up.

- It should allow you to create your own meta tags for each web page and also fully customised title tags for each web page.

- It should allow complete customisation of HTML title tags.

- It should be able to create static, rewritable and keyword-inclusive URLs instead of using dynamic parameters.

- It should provide simple administration interface and easy extensions for extra functionality.

- It should allow customisable navigation for SEO purposes.

- It should prevent duplicate content on web pages with different URLs and offer 301 redirect functionality.

- It should offer customisable robots.txt management, image naming and alt tags for images.

- It should offer efficient full site search. Make sure that it indexes the site often so that the fresh pages show up in the search results.

- If you plan to use languages other than English, then make sure that the CMS has the required multilingual character support.

Optimising the home page

The home page is perhaps the most important page on your website. It is akin to the 30-second elevator pitch about what your company is and what it does. Just as people judge others by their first impressions and the books by covers, they judge websites by their home pages. So you need to pay a lot of attention to your home page to make sure that it is effective in achieving its intended purpose.

- While there are design-related and marketing-related concerns regarding home page optimisation, the experience tells us that marketing-related concerns should be given prominence. After all, the purpose of a website (company websites, at least) is to make money, not to express your artistic creativity.

- If your company site is a one-offer site that sells only one product, then optimise it the same way as a landing page.

- Avoid trying to do too many things on the home page. You need to think hard about all the objectives you wish to achieve with the home page. Then separate them into the primary objective, major objectives and minor objectives. Three or four is enough.

- Weigh your objectives carefully and get the right mix. If you focus too much on branding rich imagery then perhaps you need to cut down space for content. If you want to optimise the page for conversions then you might need to give priority to value proposition rather than aesthetics.

- Managing your competing objectives is essential. Some of the most common objectives that claim a stake on the prime real estate of home page are branding, general site navigation, providing product tour, providing product trials and downloads, testimonials from the previous customers, existing customer login, live support and chat, newsletter sign-up, listing of all the products and services offered by the company, providing more detailed information about the products, options to buy, third party credibility symbols, secondary links to downloads and free trials, links to corporate blog and resources, images related to products and branding and social media information.

- Identify your objectives and prioritise them. Then manage and sequence them. Too many objectives and too many calls to action disorient the visitors and pull them in different directions. Give importance to marketing-related objectives such as lead generation and product trail as they are the ones that get you revenue.

- Do not assume that people know what you are and what you do. Introduce yourself and what you offer to the visitors. Start a conversation to build a relationship with the users at the home page itself.

- While podcasts and videos have their own utility value, do not completely rely on them to make your unique value proposition on the home page. Visitors may not stay long enough to check out the videos. Use text to communicate your value and then multimedia to expand on that proposition.

- Present your most important information above the fold, that is, the space of the web page you can view without having to scroll downwards.

- Test your home page. Depending on the objectives to which your home page was optimised, design key success indicators and track the progress. If the lead capturing is your primary objective then perhaps a combination of click-through rate, number of leads and number of conversions will give you an idea of how effective your home page was in achieving its objective. Likewise, define metrics and test the home page to improve and optimise it.
- The ultimate test of any home page is the number of conversions. If your conversion ratio falls below its potential, then perhaps you should redefine your objectives and redesign your home page to make it more effective.

Optimising landing pages

The purpose of a landing page is to convert visitors to sales leads and achieve sales transactions. Two types of landing pages are popular on the web – the reference landing page and the transactional landing page.

The reference landing page presents all the relevant information necessary for the visitors to make a purchase decision. The transactional landing page tries to persuade the visitor to complete a transaction such as filling out a form or giving a phone number before going into the next stage of the sales cycle.

While both styles of landing page design have their own pros and cons, reference style landing pages suit most products and services offered by small businesses.

Landing pages need not necessarily be long-copy, single product and specialised web pages that are distinct from your website. Any page you use to start a conversation with visitors is a landing page. In fact, many marketers do not use specialised landing pages and rely on the general website for sales conversions.

The purpose of a landing page is to address the traffic received from a specific and narrow channel with a single call to action. It is tailored to the needs, expectations and intentions of the traffic it receives. For example, a site visitor coming from a search engine results page is a different stage of the sales cycle than someone arriving on your web page by clicking on a pay per click ad.

Here are some smart ideas to optimise the landing pages to achieve better conversions.

- It is a myth that a landing page needs to have long copy. A longer copy does not necessarily persuade a visitor to buy your product. In fact, it might turn him off. So avoid unnecessarily lengthy landing pages.
- Tailor your content to the kind of visitors you receive. If you are optimising the landing page for visitors coming from PPC networks then you should focus on the same value proposition you offered in the ad. If the traffic is coming from social media, then perhaps you should focus on building trust and further information that takes the visitors to the next level of sales cycle.
- Instead of focusing on optimising the words or images, you should try to build a fluid sequence of thoughts that lead visitors down the desired path. Understand that it's not about pitching your product forcefully but managing a conversation that goes on in the mind of the customer.
- The value of the action you want your visitor to make should outweigh the perceived cost in performing that action. The cost of taking an action is not just punching credit card numbers but also involves time, attention, mental and physical exertion in dealing with the web page and the psychological resistance the visitor faces before submitting any personal information.
- You should a take a two-pronged approach of minimising friction and increasing the perceived value of your product or service.
- Poor aesthetic design of the landing page, lack of third party credibility indicators, poorly composed text, complexity in navigation and other annoying features of a page add to friction in the mind of the visitor. Competing objectives also increase friction. So avoid unnecessarily lengthy copy, needless form filling and distracting images to minimise friction.

- Increasing the value of the offering has more to do with increasing the *perceived* value rather than the *real* value, though the latter is very important to sustain the business in the long term.

- One way to increase the appeal of your product is to differentiate it from other competing products. Use clear and specific copy to drill your differentiating aspect into the heads of visitors.

- Another way is to increase the credibility of the product. This can be done by a variety of ways such as using testimonials, money back guarantees, intelligent copy that uses convincing numbers, magazine reviews and by displaying third party credibility symbols.

- Using numbers, quoting facts and paraphrasing positive magazine reviews are well-known ways to build credibility. Use testimonials and guarantees at the anxiety points, that is, the places on the page where visitors are likely to be anxious in performing an action such as form filling or entering credit card information.

- The design aspects of landing pages are very important in reducing friction. The visual language of the page should direct the visitors' attention to the desired path. Avoid using unnecessary images and clutter that increases friction. For example, displaying an ad or an image that adds no value right in the eye path of the visitor who just crossed the part of the page that presents your unique value proposition is a poor page design.

- If your site offers many products such as an e-retailing site then navigational aspects of the page design are very important. In fact, every page featuring a product is a landing page. You need to make it easy for your customers to jump from one product to another in a very fluid way.

Using your blog smartly

Many businesses understand the value in using blogs to communicate with their customers about a range of things such as new services, product launches, discounts, events, news and other updates. A blog is not a monologue. It is a two-way interactive communication that seeks to engage the visitors at a more personal level than a website.

A blog is also a great opportunity to establish your expert status and improve your credibility in the minds of visitors. By syndicating and tagging your blog posts across the social media sphere, you not only attract traffic but also increase the visibility of your business. Here are some tips on how you can use your blog in a better way to achieve a range of business objectives –

- A lot of businesses publish a few blog posts in the beginning with much enthusiasm but over time, they lose interest in it and they either stop posting new posts or the frequency of posting is very irregular.

- Keep publishing regular blog posts without worrying about the number of people who read them. As the word spreads and your other traffic generation campaigns pick up steam the number of visitors will automatically increase.

- Let readers post their comments. It helps to know how people perceive your views and makes the conversation interactive. There will be a few inflammatory comments but perhaps you should tolerate them to a certain level as controversy often spices up traffic.

- Keep monitoring your online reputation. If you are delegating the job of writing blog posts to one of your employees then make sure that he or she completely understands what you want to communicate with the audience and the bounds within which that communication should take place. See that the views expressed by the writer do not conflict with the views of the organisation.

- A lot of small business owners come to us and ask 'what should I blog about?' To many people their businesses are so obvious that they don't find anything interesting to write about. That is not true. If you are one of them, then perhaps you should start observing the conversations you strike with your customers, employees, suppliers, retailers and other stakeholders. You can use them to find something to write about in your blog. A blog is just like a conversation.

- Another way to identify the things to write is to observe your competition. See what they are doing and what they are writing about. Perhaps you should write about your own take on those issues.

- Keep an eye on what happens in your industry. Read the news and press releases of all important players in your market segment. Observe what various industry associations related to your market say. They provide ample opportunities to comment on.

- Always tag your blog posts and place them in appropriate categories. This helps readers to find out things related to a post without having to use the search function.

- Post various links to industry associations, government resources, community connections and non-competing peers on blogrolls. Blogroll is a group of links displayed on the sidebar of the blog's main page. Contrary to what many people think, blogrolls do not take away your traffic but increase your connectivity.

- Use RSS feed tools to let your visitors know of the latest posts. RSS (Real Simple Syndication) is a web-based tool that catches your latest post and distributes it to subscribers.

- Always post social networking and social bookmarking chiclets with every post to make it easy for your visitors to tag and spread them around on the web.

- Keep the tone of writing casual without overdoing it. A company or corporate blog is different from a personal blog. You can be informal, authentic and honest but still be professional.

- Avoid writing essays and bombarding your readers with in-your-face pitching of your products and services. A blog is not a brochure.

- Respond to the comments made by your readers. Offer additional information. Make it interactive and over the time you will be able to build a community.

Smarter online video marketing

Many businesses still do not completely exploit the power of the online video phenomenon. Video is the most powerful medium for communication and can engage the audience in a much deeper way than text and images. Videos have been proven to be effective in lowering barriers to online purchasing.

Different companies use online videos for different purposes. Depending on the nature of your business, you can also use videos to achieve a variety of objectives such as –

1. **Enhancing brand awareness**. Instead of or apart from making videos on each product you can build videos to push the brand much like traditional marketing.
2. **Product advertising**. Create informative and educational videos about your products and services. Highlight their unique features. Focus on what viewers can connect through visuals and include a lot of close-up shots of your products.
3. **Retail promotion**. Videos are a great tool to advertise short term promotions such as weekend sales or special discount offers.
4. **Direct sales promotion**. Some products are best promoted by showing them in action such as machines or brand new apartments. Make sure that you include your contact details and lead capture information at the end of the video.
5. **Videos for product support**. You can create short training videos that focus on how to use various features of your products and post them on net. In some ways, it is far easier to explain some things by showing them rather than writing about them.
6. **Connecting with customers**. You can post videos of your or your CEO's speeches, company seminars and other presentations that provide useful and interesting information to the former and potential customers.

In spite of all the hype surrounding online video marketing, many small businesses still do not give it the attention it deserves. To make the most of the power of video marketing, follow these tactics –

- Do not isolate the video experience. Some websites still use a video section or a separate '.tv' domain to place their promotional and informative video clips. Since they are isolated from the natural path the customer follows on the website, they are not effective. Always embed your videos in your main website in an appropriate way.
- Avoid playing your videos automatically when the web page is opened. It irritates the viewers and makes them leave the page without even bothering to stop the video.
- Use common video formats such as flash. Do not force your viewers to download a special plug-in to view your videos.
- Make it easy to play the video. Try to post videos at lower resolutions (240p or 360p). Resolutions higher than this do not enhance the viewer experience in any significant way. On the other hand, it increases download times and streaming interruptions. A better alternative is to upload videos with a choice for viewers to select the resolution.
- Embed the video into page instead of having to open a separate page or go to an outside video-hosting site. Always optimise the context around the video with necessary description, keywords and other related content.
- Always enable video sharing and distribute the video on the web using various practices of social media optimisation. To make the most of any video, you need to make it viral.
- The videos you produce do not have to be slick. In fact, being amateurish makes the right connection with the audience. Keep your videos short, almost always under 5 minutes.

Mobile-enabled version of a website

The mobile phone is personal and is always carried. People almost always check their messages. So any promotional SMS you send is nearly sure to be viewed. With the proliferation of the wireless internet, many mobile users now access the web through their mobile handsets.

However, the internet is built with the personal computer in mind. Mobile users access web pages in far smaller screens and have far less navigational ease compared to PC users. The low bandwidth and low memory of mobile devices is also an impediment.

If mobile marketing forms an important part of your marketing mix and if there is a significant proportion of customers who access your site via mobile devices, then you should seriously consider creating a mobile version of your website.

People using mobile devices to access your site are more likely to be task-specific and purpose-driven. These two aspects need to be taken into consideration while building a mobile version of the site.

Mobile users are also time-sensitive. They are unlikely to spend hours browsing as their PC counterparts do. To many users accessing your site via mobiles, location plays an important role. The most accessed information usually relates to their location such as restaurants, cinema theatres, etc.

Here are some tips to build effective mobile versions of websites that greatly help in improving the user experience.

- Keep it simple. No unnecessary images, videos and flash animations.
- Navigation is important. Place the necessary links at the top and bottom of the each page to make it easy for the user to go to another page.
- All images and logos should be attractive but as small file size as possible. If it is more than 2 KB then perhaps you should look for another image.
- People on the go do not have much time for reading articles that are long and seem to have no end. For mobile users, reduce your articles to bullet points and easily digestible chunks.

- By analysing the previous traffic and most accessed pages, you would be able to tell what services and information is of most importance to mobile users. Provide such information and services on the first page itself.
- Always check your mobile website. There are many tools such as mobiReady[1], W3C mobileOK checker[2] and Mobile Web Practices 1.0[3] which help you make sure that everything is in order.
- Aggressively promote the URL of your mobile website. Place it along with the general version URL in every promotional material you use.

Capturing leads and generating sales

Capturing leads and generating sales or contacts are the ultimate marketing objectives of any website. Everything you expend on conceiving, designing and maintaining a website needs to focus on achieving these objects. Apart from the various techniques discussed about optimising various elements of a website, here are some more recommendations that help you capture more leads, generate more sales and optimise your site as a whole.

- Focus on one primary objective and two or three secondary objectives. If there are more objectives then you are probably trying to accomplish too much and the results could be counterproductive.
- What unique value proposition are you making? Is your website clearly presenting that proposition to visitors? Why should your customer buy the product from you when there are so many other competitors? Most websites fail because business owners have no clarity on their value proposition. Think deeply about this.
- After you are done with all the designing and preparation of the website, look at the home page and assess its impact. Is your home page capable of strongly 'hooking' the visitor in the first six or seven seconds? If your answer is

---

[1] http://ready.mobi/launch.jsp?locale=en_EN
[2] http://validator.w3.org/mobile/
[3] http://www.w3.org/TR/mobile-bp/

negative, then perhaps you should rethink your website design strategy.

- A lot of visitors are not likely to have any kind of commitment when they first visit your website. Your site should be able to engage and take them through successive levels of involvement. Check and make sure that the content, appearance, site structure and other elements of the site do this in a fluid manner.

- To capture leads and to move them through incremental levels of commitment demands –
  1. clear lead capturing
  2. presenting the necessary information in an interesting way
  3. educating about products and services through articles, eBooks and other information delivery channels
  4. special notifications, clearance sales, discounts and other purchase opportunities
  5. credible and safe purchase transaction facility that gains confidence of your prospects

- How strong are your credibility indicators? Testimonials, awards, endorsements, certifications, third-party ratings, survey findings and other media recognition enhance your credibility and increase conversions.

- Present the options and calls to action to your customers in a logical sequential way. Too much clutter can increase friction and mess with decision-making.

- How appealing is the design? How are various chunks of information organised on the screen? How is the site organised? These questions help you assess the design aspects of the website.

- The copy of the site should flow naturally and rhyme with the thought processes occurring in the minds of your prospects. Content should be psychologically ergonomic.

- A good copy emphasises the problem or an opportunity with incisive questions and presents a workable solution. The solution is presented in such a logical way that it corresponds to the mental processes of the prospect's purchase decision making process – namely, doubt about the solution, understanding the solution, explanation of the solution, illustration or demonstration of the solution and proof.

- Finally the solution is summarised and a strong call to action is made to persuade the prospect to take the desired action.

Chapter 6
Using Tools to Automate Your Marketing

Sending the right message to the right customer at the right time is the mantra of marketing success. Following up with your leads is essential to your business and many small businesses have no idea how marketing automation software applications can improve their productivity. These applications make things simple and easy for you by automating and centralising mundane tasks such as billing, database management, starting a dialogue and sending periodic marketing literature to your customers. They help you grow your business without having to hire more staff.

Overview of automated marketing

Generating leads and following them up with persuasive literature to gain their confidence to make a purchase decision is the essence of marketing. Once you have set up your website and begin to get leads, you need to focus on nurturing them to turn them into customers.

A lot of small business owners are too focused on getting new traffic and new leads. That is good but they do not invest the same amount of psychological energy on their existing leads. The whole process of managing the contact details of leads, sending them periodic literature, delivering emails, sending offline marketing literature, managing affiliates, managing subscriptions and processing payments can be a tedious and mundane job. Add to this the new social media channels and the need to create and distribute content across them on a regular basis. It is no wonder that many small business owners do not have sufficient time and expertise to do it all by themselves.

This is where automated marketing systems come into the picture. These applications make your life easy without having to add more staff to your organisation. They simplify things by automating many repetitive processes. You can specify criteria and outcomes for various tasks and the software application executes them according to your specifications. This reduces human error and increases the efficiency in a great way.

Marketing workflow automation in large companies may include automating a large proportion of internal marketing processes right from budgeting and planning to enterprise-wide customer relationship management.

However, for small business owners, the most important automation functions are lead management, lead scoring and lead nurturing, periodic delivery of pre-defined sales literature, email marketing, social media content distribution and payment processing.

Why do you need marketing automation applications?

Marketing automation applications focus on managing your leads by targeting them with pre-designed content to increase awareness and interest in your products and services. They nurture your leads from the first interest through to the sale.

There are three types of leads in every business. Hot leads or the prospects who want to buy your products right now. They know what they want and they have very high motivation levels and have decided to buy.

The second type of leads is called warm leads. They are interested in your product but they are not yet ready to punch their credit card numbers. They have medium motivation levels. They are just checking out what your product really is but have not made up their mind.

Warm leads form a huge proportion of all leads and as any experienced businessperson will tell you, they are very important. If you depend solely on hot leads, then your business will not be able to sustain for long. You need to nurture the warm leads, follow them up with information regarding your offerings, increase their motivation levels and gain their confidence to make the deal.

The third type of leads is cold deals or the lead that may never mature into a deal. These are the people who are part of traffic that bumped into your website. These are the people who are just looking for information with no intention of buying.

The problem is it is very difficult to know which lead is warm and which one is cold. Another problem is timing. Even if you happen to identify the warm leads, you need to time your marketing information delivery to their motivation levels. You need to be able to send the right message at the right time.

Your business might have a lot of business literature such as brochures, invitation letters, articles, product information, discount sale offers and other items. You are going to need a system that can deliver the right kind of message to your leads at the right time without fail. Understand that people buy when they are ready to buy or when they feel like buying, not when you are ready to sell.

Repeat business is very important for any business which wants to remain for the long term. Considering the proportion of up-selling and cross-selling to existing customers, then it becomes even more apparent that nurturing your leads and previous customers is a must.

To be in touch with your customers, you need to maintain a customer database. Without a database, you cannot identify your previous customers and it's as if you will have to start the process all over again with every lead.

By entering all the details, including order and billing info, of your customers, leads and prospects, you can organise your customers into meaningful groups and target them with appropriate loyalty and follow-up programs.

Marketing automation helps you in many ways, such as –

- It stores all the important details about your prospects, leads and customers which you can use for a variety of purposes.
- It lets you communicate with your prospects in an efficient manner as opposed to traditional one-on-one communication which is time-consuming.
- You can send regular information to your prospects and target them in a variety of ways for multiple purposes.
- Since a large part of communication is repetitive (sending a welcome email upon first registration, sending the first brochure or free report, sending the details about other related products and services), making it automatic saves a lot of time and energy.
- You can track the progress of your marketing and sales programs.

Using an email autoresponder system

The most important feature of a marketing automation software application is its email autoresponder. You can set up content (such as welcome emails, confirmation emails, special reports sent at regular intervals, etc.) and set them to deliver automatically.

You can use them for customer follow-up. As soon as a prospect enters his or her email address on your website's lead capture form, email autoresponder can be set up to send a welcome email. The email might present a general introduction of what your business does and how the products or services can help them. You might also send further links to free reports or white papers or other educational materials.

You can set the autoresponder to send a series of emails with promotional material at predefined intervals of time. For example, on the immediate day of the email registration you can send a welcome email along with a link to download free reports.

When the prospect downloads the report from your website, another email can be set to send thanking the prospect for downloading the report. The same email may also contain further links or information on what your product or service can do for the prospects. This can be made even more effective if you send out client case studies and testimonials in which other businesses sing your praises.

If the customer clicks on the link to find more about product, you might send an email with more details such as pricing and discount options.

The next day, another email with a promotional discount offer can be sent with the discount set to expire in a certain number of days.

You can follow-up customers with periodic informational articles. This is also called drip marketing. Even if the prospect shows no interest in the initial days, you should be sending marketing literature at regular intervals, at least once every two weeks, to stay in touch with the prospects. It has been proven that it can take up to 8 contacts between a business and prospects before a transaction occurs. Don't make a pest of yourself but also don't give up too quickly on leads that may just need more information or a little time before they trust you enough to do business with you.

Email autoresponders can send thousands of emails in a matter of minutes which would be impossible for you to type and deliver one by one.

If your business processes orders online, then email autoresponder can be set to send standard emails detailing billing information and order confirmation. This helps to make your prospects feel comfortable and increases the trust factor.

If you publish any new articles or offer new reports and white papers, you can let your customers know about them by sending announcement emails.

Customer segmentation using marketing automation

Marketing automation applications let you segment your prospects so that you can target them more effectively. Once your prospects sign up, you can segment them by the details they have given in the lead capture forms, the emails clicked and opened, the kind of articles and reports they have downloaded from your website, the kind of products and services they previously purchased.

Such segmentation helps you target your prospects with the promotional literature that best suits them. Hyper-targeting your customers with smart marketing campaigns help you nurture your prospects and improve your sales over time.

Make sure that you send only relevant information that your prospect is likely to use. It decreases unsubscribe rates and increases loyalty.

Choosing an autoresponder system

With so many autoresponder and marketing automation software applications on the market, it can be difficult to choose the one that best fits your needs. Here are few pointers that will help you select the best application.

- **Personalised response** – Make sure that your email autoresponder allows significant personalisation. Your customer needs to feel that the email has been sent by a human instead of a program.

- **Check the text length** – Make sure that the program allows enough text length to meet your needs. It is best to go for the one that allows unlimited text in emails.

- **Automatic follow-ups** – The application should have the option to set automatic follow-up of emails without having to need manual interaction.

- **Automatic notification** – The application should let you track the performance of your campaigns. When a prospect requests information, you should be immediately notified of that request.

- **Scalability** – Many marketing automation applications put limits on the number of contact details and the number of emails that can be sent in a campaign (usually in thousands). As your business increases you should have the option to scale up the number of contacts and emails by paying the required amounts but without having to switch the plan altogether.

- **Deliverability** – With email deliverability an increasing issue in these days of large amounts of email spam you need to ensure you choose a reputable service. Look for one that is certified with Return Path who have very stringent qualification standards. At the very least ensure that you run all your emails through a spam filter to be sure you are not inadvertently using terms that could be construed as spam.

Integration with SMS for mobile follow-up

Mobile marketing is an increasingly popular form of communication. Research reveals that while the open rate of emails is about 26%, for text messages it is 97%. To make the best use of marketing automation, you need to integrate mobile marketing with other forms of marketing.

The application should be able to use SMS to follow up with your prospects. While some applications do not provide in-built SMS integration, you can find third party apps that can do so. Integrating SMS into marketing automation has many benefits such as –

- It simplifies your marketing campaigns across platforms. Now you can manage two different marketing campaigns from the same application.

- You can integrate the results too. For example, when someone opens up an SMS and opts to download coupons, you can follow the same prospect with an email offering further details about the related products and services.

- For many small businesses which depend on time-sensitive discount sales and special offers, SMS alerts work better than email campaigns. For example, an SMS alert is more likely to be effective than an email campaign when a local pub offers a weekend discount.

- SMS alerts work best for certain industries such as hotels, airplane reservations and restaurants, etc., where there is little to educate your customers but specific information is very valuable such as booking reservations for a concert or restaurant.

- SMS integration can also be used to distribute important alerts and announcements, to send subscription forms into websites, accepting new subscribers and removing unsubscribers, to communicate special offers to customers and create customer loyalty and trust by staying in touch.

- SMS short codes are also worth using to make it easier to capture leads on the move. Typically these work by allowing users to opt in by texting their name or email and a keyword and short code number

Integration with a mailing house for postcard follow-up

Using advanced marketing automation software applications, you can link your marketing activities across multiple platforms into one well-oiled machine. For example, the very first day a prospect registers on your website, you can send a welcome email.

The same day, the details of the contact are forwarded to an offline print fulfilment house which will follow-up with a printed free report or white paper that is delivered in two or three days. On the fourth day, you can set an email to be sent to the prospect with the details of the offline report sent.

You can coordinate online as well as offline marketing campaigns from the same platform. The application also makes it easy for you to design and manage contact details of the prospects for both online and mailing house campaigns. It lets you engage your prospects at multiple touch points such as mail, SMS, postcard and fax, etc.

Some examples of marketing automation applications

Here are some of the most popular marketing applications for small businesses.

Infusionsoft (http://www.infusionsoft.com)

Even if you have never set up an email marketing campaign, Infusionsoft can help you manage your marketing campaigns very efficiently in a small amount of time. It helps small businesses and entrepreneurs improve their productivity and boost their sales.

Infusionsoft is more than an email autoresponder, it is a high-end customer relationship management application with which you can track everything about your leads. Every time your prospect clicks on a link or opens an email or downloads a special report from your site, Infusionsoft tracks and uses that data to create segmented lists of prospects which can be used to send highly targeted marketing campaigns.

It lets you set up specific rules to send specific messages to prospects based on their preferences at predetermined intervals of time. Such smart automation helps you deliver relevant messages to right prospects at the right time.

The application programming interface (API) of Infusionsoft lets you integrate your database with multiple platforms such as your website, blog, Twitter, FaceBook and others.

OfficeAutoPilot (http://officeautopilot.com)

OfficeAutoPilot is an all-in-one marketing automation platform designed for small businesses. It integrates contact management, automated marketing, payment processing, automated tasks execution and even affiliate marketing.

It helps you follow up your prospects, both online and offline, with automated predetermined multi-setup sequences of marketing message delivery. You can sell your offerings, manage the subscriptions and process payments very easily.

You can collect and analyse all the information about your prospects and clients in a single online system. With the email marketing delivery tools and offline mail follow up system, you can target your prospects with relevant messages.

AWeber (http://www.aweber.com)

AWeber is a professional email marketing tool that has helped many businesses. It lets you collect, manage and segment your prospects by the details provided by them.

One of the interesting features of AWeber is its collection of over 150 HTML email templates which you can use to make your emails look richer and appealing. You can set flexible rules in the email autoresponder to deliver a sequence of emails to your prospects automatically.

The strong email analytics feature lets you track the performance of email marketing campaigns by many parameters such as who opened the mails, how many links were clicked, number of people unsubscribed and the revenue generated by each message.

Hootsuite (http://hootsuite.com)

Hootsuite is a social media dashboard which allows you to view and post content to multiple social media channels from one central location. This can be a big time saver compared with having to repeatedly log in to multiple social media accounts. Among others you can use it to update Twitter, FaceBook Pages, LinkedIn and WordPress.

Here is a list of other popular marketing automation software applications you can use to manage your campaigns.

GetResponse (http://www.getresponse.com)

Constant Contact (http://www.constantcontact.com)

1ShoppingCart (http://www.1shoppingcart.com)

MailChimp (http://www.mailchimp.com)

Benchmark Email (http://www.benchmarkemail.com)

How to get more contacts into my database

As you can see, marketing automation is all about managing your customer database and social media followers and following them up with regular marketing messages designed to heighten their purchase intent. The more contacts and followers you have, the greater your chances in making more conversions.

There needs to be a lead development and lead capture strategy in place. For a website, a web form asking for email address is the most frequently used contact generation strategy. With the onslaught of spam menace, people think twice before giving away their email details. They become even more suspicious when asked for phone number and home address. Normally, the first name, last name and email address suffice for contact generation.

The best way to entice leads and develop contacts is to give something away for free. Some of the most effective lead generation incentives are contests, coupons, discounts, free trials, free webinars, free reports and whitepapers and other downloadable content such as software applications, music, audio and videos.

Here are three ideas to get more contacts in exchange for information –

Digital Products from Kunaki (http://kunaki.com) Kunaki is a DVD and CD automation firm that lets you publish CDs and DVDs at very low prices. Offering a free or low priced CD stuffed with information useful to the prospects is an effective way to get more details such as home address and phone number.

If you are wondering about the costs associated with DVD and CD publishing then look no further than Kunaki. It offers many benefits to small businesses in that you don't have to incur any upfront costs or inventory or other risks.

You can configure your digital product online by including content such as eBooks, information, audio, video and software downloads. You can design your product virtually including the disc, case, cover art, inserts and content. It takes just one day to get your product to market. In effect, you can publish your digital product at no cost.

Once created you can automate the fulfilment of these products to be sent out to your leads directly.

Free Reports and Whitepapers. One other way to get more contacts is to offer your visitors free reports and whitepapers. Offering information that is useful and educative usually entices prospects to give their email address to you.

To engage with your audience you need to create marketing literature beforehand. It could be few special reports or whitepapers or manuals or free guides that have some use apart from information value.

You can configure your marketing automation application to deliver these reports and whitepapers automatically as soon as a visitor signs up in the web form on your site. Then you can follow up with further reports and articles at regular intervals to educate your prospects.

Videos. People like to watch video content. Videos also make people stay longer on your site. Research indicates that watching online videos can lower friction and heighten purchase intent.

By creating a secure members area where registered members can have access to premium video content, you can get more contacts and build a strong community. The activities of some businesses need more demonstration rather than explanation. For example, if you are local real estate broker, perhaps you can shoot videos of your properties for sale and post them on the web.

By asking for contact details before people sign up to watch your content, you can get more leads and follow them up with more marketing messages whenever new products come up in your inventory.

You can also use FaceBook to generate fans. By running FaceBook adverts that closely target the demographics of your ideal customer you can entice them to like your page by offering free information. Again this can be automated using scripts that automatically deliver items to your fans as soon as they click the like button on your page.

Chapter 7

Educating Your Prospects and Customers

It is said that marketing is nothing but education. Unless your prospects know what you are, what your products can do for them and why they need your services, they will not buy from you. You need to educate your prospects and customers by following them up with regular and information-rich marketing messages. By targeting your content to the buyers' decision-making cycle, you can lead them through various levels of purchase intention and finally gain their confidence to make the 'buy' decision.

Why you need to educate your prospects and customers?

Not all leads are hot and you will have to cultivate warm leads to gain business down the line. Depending solely on hot leads and directing all your marketing efforts toward them can be very expensive and counterproductive.

Not all customers come to you with the same mindset. Different prospects are at different stages of the buying cycle. The level of interest, their purchase intent, the immediacy of the need of your product, presence of competing products, availability of substitute products, pricing and the financial capability are only a few factors that affect people's buying behaviour.

If your marketing campaigns target only those at the end of the sales funnel, then you are not going to make as many sales as you could. You need to engage other prospects who are at varying levels of purchase intent and follow them up with regular information-rich marketing messages.

When you educate your prospects and customers –

1. You increase the brand awareness and brand recall which will help you when they finally make a decision to buy.
2. Since many leads mature to become customers over time, your business gets more business than you would have if you depend solely on hot leads.
3. By staying in touch with your customers, you can up-sell and cross-sell more products and services to your existing customers.
4. To get the sales you need to make your prospects overcome their psychological barrier and friction. Educating your prospects increases your credibility and trust factor and the prospects will be more willing to buy from you.

Educating your prospects need not be a tedious and time-consuming process. By using marketing automation applications and email autoresponders, you can stay in touch with your prospects and put in place ongoing follow-up campaigns that are automatic.

Online follow-up campaigns using email news-letters

Email newsletters are extremely cost-effective with very low cost per contact. They are highly targeted and at the same time customisable on a large scale. They are completely measurable and their performance can be tracked very accurately.

As with any marketing campaign, you need to plan your email newsletter follow-up with care to get the best results. You need to analyse, optimise and then keep fine-tuning the campaign to achieve your goals. Here are some important things you need to remember while devising and executing any email campaign.

1. Once you have the list of required contacts to which the emails are to be sent, define the goals of your campaign. This helps to analyse and track the effectiveness of the campaign.
2. Most common goals of email campaigns are making leads purchase your product or having a certain number of downloads, say of a whitepaper, from your website or to get a certain number of requests for further information or to improve the number of people signing up for free trials.
3. Depending on the goals you have had in mind, identify the key performance indicators that will help you understand your performance. Open rate of emails, click-through rate, number of emails forwarded, number of clicks on landing pages, the total ROI on the campaign are some metrics you can use.
4. You campaign can only be as effective as your lists. The quality of contacts is the most important determinant of the conversion ratio achieved at the end of any email campaign. Try to get as many quality leads as possible.
5. Spam menace has made life difficult for many email marketers. Make sure that you have the permission of the contact to send a promotional email. Check all the legal

obligations you need to adhere to when sending marketing emails.

6. Double opt-in emails are the best ones to have. Provide lead generation incentives such as free reports and whitepapers to persuade people to give you their email details and permission to send emails.

7. State your anti-spam policy very clearly in the sign-up page and use a strong call to action. Clearly explain the nature of the content in the emails you will be sending and the benefits of receiving those emails. Always include unsubscribe option in your emails. Avoid asking too many details unless necessary.

8. Emails can be rendered by web browsers as either text emails or HTML emails. Text emails, as the name suggests, contain only text while HTML emails can contain text, images, hyperlinks and rich formatting with various fonts and colours. However, some email service providers such as Gmail turn off displaying images in HTML emails by default. Users have to turn on image display to view any images contained in such mails.

9. Your emails need to have a header, footer, subject line, personalised greeting, body where your marketing message resides and an unsubscribe link.

10. Using marketing automation applications described in the previous chapter you can easily create attractive email newsletters. Many such applications contain hundreds of templates to choose from. You can just add your company name and other details and make your emails look very professional.

11. Since different people would be receiving emails on different platforms, you need to test your mails for compatibility and deliverability. Use any of the free online spam score checkers[1] to make sure that your email is not considered as spam by webmail service providers.

12. The marketing message you deliver should be consistent across all promotional platforms. Whether it is an email or offline printed brochure, the message needs to have similar tone, clarity and content.

---

[1] http://spamcheck.sitesell.com/ and
http://www.contactology.com/check_mqs.php

13. Many marketing automation platforms allow customisation. Depending on the personal information offered by prospects and their prior behaviour you can segment your prospects into various lists to be targeted by more meaningful and relevant messages.

14. Transaction emails such as order confirmation mails and shipping notification emails are a great opportunity to cross-promote other related and relevant products and services.

15. How frequently should you be sending an email to your prospects is subject to debate but one thing we are sure of is you should be sending a lot. However, make sure that you are sending something that is useful and has information value. Note that many prospects skip a significant number of emails you send without even bothering to open them.

16. The analytics associated with marketing automation software applications will generate a lot of reports that will help you track, analyse and optimise your campaigns. Number of emails delivered, number of bounces, bounce rate, emails opened, hyperlinks clicked, click-through rate, unsubscribe rate, emails forwarded and the conversions from email traffic are some performance indicators that should give you a complete picture of your performance. Use the information to make your email marketing messages more relevant and useful.

17. Once you are done with sending emails, expect an onrush of requests, calls and orders. Make sure that your business systems and processes can handle the traffic.

How to write great email newsletters

Many email recipients take no more than two seconds to decide whether to open an email newsletter and read it. So it is imperative that you grab their attention and hook them to the email right from the subject line itself.

Subject Lines. Make your subject line interesting and captivating. Your subject line needs to provide the hook to keep them from straying away. One oft-used way to generate interest is to ask a question. When you ask someone a question, their mind naturally looks for an answer. It is a natural reflex. Consider the following email newsletter for a subject line.

Are you making the most of your internet traffic?

The question 'Are you making the most of your internet traffic?' instantly makes readers think whether they are making full use of the internet traffic they are receiving at their site. Their brain automatically supplies them with some answers such as 'yes', 'no', and 'may be not as much as I want'.

Another way to come up with interesting subject lines is to provide doubt or uncertainty. Human minds have little tolerance for uncertainty and ambiguity. They need to be sure that they are sure about something, even if it happens to be far from the truth.

Once you have a strong subject line you need to continue with strong copy. Consider the following as the introductory paragraph.

If you are not gathering info about your visitors you are probably losing thousands of dollars every year. Boost your profits up to 500% by building opt-in lists.

In the first paragraph above, pay attention to the part – 'If you are not gathering info about your visitors you are probably losing thousands of dollars every year'. Instilling doubt and creating uncertainty about not being able to earn more money because of not gathering info about customers works at a subtle level and captures their attention, which, of course, is all you need to hook them to the page.

Taken to the extreme, you can even instil fear in the minds of the people. This tactic is very popular in healthcare sector. For example, 'Which would you rather have, a cholesterol test or an autopsy?' tries to scare people into taking a cholesterol test.

Another way to grab attention is to offer a benefit. '30% discount sale', 'boost your profits up by 500%' and 'improve your revenues by 40%' all fall in this category. If you are offering anything else that benefits the reader, then include it in the subject line. It appeals to the natural greed of the human beings and arrests their attention.

Always end your email with a call to action verb such as 'Join Now'. A call to action tells the reader what to do. After the reader has gone through the title or the content of the newsletter, he needs to be told what to do next in as clear language as possible. 'Click here', 'Join now' and 'Sign up now for a free trial' are all examples of calls to action.

But avoid creating too much hype. When you fail to deliver on what you promised in the subject line, you lose credibility and it becomes very hard to convince the people the next time you send a newsletter.

Bullet Points and Short Paragraphs. People kind of scan through material at a fast pace on the web rather than read it thoroughly, as say in a textbook. Keeping your paragraphs short and using bullet points helps them very much.

A paragraph should ideally have no more than 50 words. Shorter the better. Small paragraphs are easy to read and understand. Follow the golden rule of advertisement copywriting – one paragraph for one idea.

Use bullet lists when describing the potential benefits and features of your products and services. Scanning the bullets alone should drive home the marketing message you want to deliver. Another advantage of using bullet lists is they unconsciously lead readers from one point to the next.

Offer Freebies. People like free stuff. Freebies such as eBooks, special reports, how-to guides, marketing surveys, podcasts and case studies interest people and make them come back to your site.

Make sure that what you offer through these freebies has something useful and interesting to your readers. Avoid offering fluffy and outdated information.

Have a Voice. Identify topics of interest and express your opinions on them. You can even make statements that cry out for attention and are controversial as long as you don't overdo it. Challenge the accepted wisdom of people. Pose questions that make them think. Make the conversation personal.

Make it Interactive. Invite your readers to take a poll. Conduct surveys and let them know the results. People love to state their opinions and have their voices heard.

Follow-up campaigns using smartphone apps

When it comes to mobile marketing, the screen space of your customer is the most wanted real estate. With more and more people using smartphones, a mobile app is the surest way to make your mark in the market.

So what is a smartphone app? First of all, a smartphone is a mobile phone that offers advanced computing ability and is almost like a mini personal computer. A smartphone app is similar to a software application we install and use on PCs; the difference being it works on a smartphone instead of a PC.

Smartphone apps are a great way to stay in touch with your customers and increase their loyalty. There are many ways a smartphone app can be designed and used to suit your marketing objectives, especially small businesses.

With a smartphone app, a user can access all the information he or she needs right from the app instead of having to pass through many steps which become unavoidable while using a website to gain information. In essence, your smartphone app is your website in motion.

You can allow your customers to register their credit cards and store the bar code information on their mobiles using an app. You can use the purchase data to design targeted promotions that will appeal to your customers as they better address their needs and expectations.

Similarly, a restaurateur can use an app which customers can install on their mobile phones and use it to check out new menu items and make reservations. The restaurant itself can update the app advertising any special occasions and discounts.

Following up with offline campaigns

Depending on only one or two platforms to stay in touch with your prospects and customers will not help you deliver your message every time you want it. You need to develop a network of traditional as well as digital touch points to interact with your customer base.

Apart from online follow-up and mobile follow-up, you also need to kick-start offline campaigns. Flyers, postcards, brochures and printed newsletters are the traditional follow-up options you should use to drive home your marketing message.

A lot of people still like to have information in the old-fashioned way. Offline follow-up gets such customers' attention, keeps them interested, increases their purchase intent and encourages them to take the desired action.

Flyers. A flyer is made from a single sheet of paper but can have a wide variety of formats. When you have information that fills only a page then you should try flyers. They can be mailed to customers and also distributed on other offline marketing platforms such as conventions, conferences and exhibitions.

Postcards. They are cheap to produce and can be directly mailed to your prospects. They have high readerships too. Don't go for cheap paper as postcards are really small paper sheets. On the other hand, unless you are printing multi-colour, do not go for high gloss paper. Use sizes other than the standard postcard size to get attention.

Since postcards are small and there is only so much space you can use, your message must be succinct and to the point. Postcards are best to draw attention toward your products and services and to increase the intention of knowing more about them. Do not try to close sales with postcards as the space is not enough to provide enough information to convincingly close the sale.

You can also use postcards to drive leads back online by using things like personalised URLs (PURLs). By using modern variable data printing it is possible to include personal information on postcards. For example you might have a PURL which includes the users name such as www.specialoffer.com/John Smith. This highly personalised form of marketing gets good results as people see their name and are more likely to visit the link as it contains something specific for them.

Brochures. These are marketing messages printed in booklet format. Brochures are generally used to give an overview of what your company does and what its products and services are. Product-specific brochures are also used to discuss primarily a single product.

Newsletters. Printed newsletters and bulletins have an advantage over email newsletters. They don't get filtered out by spam. They get delivered. Printed newsletters have greater perceived value than email newsletters. They are real and they are tangible unlike their virtual counterparts.

While email newsletters hardly manage to get a glance from their viewers, printed versions are more likely to have greater attention from their recipients. They also get handed over to other people and passed along. They offer more convenient and comfortable reading than email newsletters. It really is hard to read for long on a computer monitor.

What if there is nothing to educate your prospects about?

Some businesses do not follow the educate-your-prospects model as there is little or nothing to educate them about. Think about pizza businesses. People want to have a pizza instead of learning about its history. Here the delivery of a great gastronomic experience is more important than intellectual stimulation.

Get found by your customers. For the kind of businesses discussed above, it still is important to stay in touch with your prospects and customers. Education may be less relevant to them but brand recall and brand awareness is very important. For a hair salon and a local pizza delivery business, to be remembered when a customer needs your service is essential.

Send notifications to your customers. Another way to make more from your existing customers is to let them know of any discounts and special sales via online and offline marketing communication platforms. Maybe you can build a list of your customers and their phone numbers and then SMS them about a weekend discount sale or new additions.

Create exclusivity. Creating exclusive products or services or experiences is a very old marketing principle. Think of ways you can make your customers feel special Exclusivity is not something related only to luxury goods. Maybe you can create a member's club where certain premium services can be offered. Maybe you can make your products and services more customised and make them available to select members.

Maybe you can identify those customers who bring the most business (think Pareto's 20-80 principle) and invite them to form a premium club. By providing members' only services, you create an aura and mystique around them. This drives their perception value and brings in more revenue.

You can even create an exclusive email list of frequent shoppers to whom you can send special discount coupons and premium offerings or private events and let them know that they are receiving the invitations as VIPs or priority customers.

How to achieve thought leadership through information-rich content

For some smart small business owners and entrepreneurs web content has a very powerful but less obvious objective. They use it to brand themselves as a thought leader. Instead of using content directly to promote their products and services they establish themselves as an expert and thought leader to whom many prospects and customers come for an advice.

To be a thought leader, you need to understand how your customers think. You need to use their words and phrases and use that information to build a very engaging and interesting relationship. You need to know the buyers' persona inside out.

Thought leadership is not about using jargon but explaining complex topics in simple layman language, in the language your prospects best understand. It is about moving beyond the paradigm of simple advertisement and product promotion.

A webinar that discusses a solution, a white paper that offers in-depth insights and an eBook that provides a detailed action plan to manage an issue – these content forms may not immediately produce a measurable effect on your sales or conversions but immensely adds to your company's positive standing and perception value.

Here is what you need to brand yourself as a thought leader in your industry –

1. Look at things not as a businessman trying to sell things but as a buyer searching for useful information. Create content that helps your prospective customers. The content may or may not have a direct relation to what you sell. In fact, you do not mention your products and services. You might design the content in such a way that people will look for your solution rather than that of any other company.
   For example, if you are a local restaurant then you might write a small eBook on 'How to Plan the Perfect Wedding

Reception?' or '50 Great Tips to Have a Romantic Evening Dinner'.

2. Publish white papers to brand yourself as an authority of your subject. A white paper is an authoritative guide that solves a problem or discusses a solution. They are widely used to help readers get in-depth information and make informed decisions.

    White papers can outline the benefits of a certain technology or methodology or solution. They can also be used to describe various aspects of how a technology or solution works.

    Look for most discussed problems in your market segment from the perspective of a client and write white papers discussing various ways those problems can be solved (of course, indirectly referring to how your company solves those problems).

    Understand that a white paper is not a brochure. While it is an accepted practice to devote a page or two at the end of the white paper to discuss your products, the white paper as a whole is not a product brochure or manual.

    Offer your white papers as a lead capture incentive on your website. Let the visitors download them freely by giving away their email address details which you can use to follow up with marketing campaigns.

3. Email newsletters are another way to achieve thought leadership. Instead of just promoting your products and services in every newsletter, focus on providing information that helps people gain a better understanding of the issues faced in your market segment. You can also send the latest news and your opinions on various events related to your business.

4. EBooks are widely used to promote organizations. It is a wonderful way to provide information to your prospects. Unlike white papers, the topics being discussed do not particularly have to be in-depth but they have to have information value. You can present even basic information regarding a subject.

    EBooks use a more personal and conversational tone in their presentation, unlike white papers which are sober and authoritative. However, just like white papers, offer them for free and use them as a lead generation tool.

5. Webinars or web-based seminars feature audio or video presentations of experts discussing various solutions to a problem. You can invite people outside your organisation and hold discussion and upload them as webinars.

6. Market research and surveys are another way many companies brand themselves as the experts. While it can be expensive to conduct primary research that is statistically significant, you can use online surveys and post those results on your website.

7. Post videos that simplify complex topics on your site. People like to watch rather than read. Videos also connect with them at a more personal level and build a more impressive relationship.

8. If you or your organisation do not have the capabilities to create such content on your own, then it is best to hire professional people. There are also many online organisations and platforms[1] where you can hire writers and programmers to create thought leadership-content.

---

[1] http://www.elance.com, http://www.odesk.com, http://www.vworker.com

Chapter 8
Putting It All Together

Online marketing is not a one-time effort. You need to integrate it into your other business processes and systems. The internet is a level playing field. Every business is lined up on the same street and markets to the same customers. To succeed in this flat world, you must create exceptional content, target your audience, deliver the right message and exceed the expectations of your customers. To do that you need to have an action plan and an ongoing process to conceive, create, manage and execute online marketing campaigns that engage your prospects at every available opportunity throughout the year.

The overall process flow

As said earlier, the fundamentals of marketing are same everywhere but when it comes to online marketing it's just the means of achieving the marketing goals which are a bit different. To be successful on internet, you need to understand the way it functions and devise effective marketing processes.

The unique nature of online marketing is its ability to let you reach global audience with minimal cost. This vastly reduces the entry cost barriers and puts small businesses at a level playing field with corporate monoliths.

While the internet has revolutionised the way we do business, many businessmen and entrepreneurs still look at it as an advertising platform. The thing is it is more than that. It is a communications medium that can be put to many uses. These include reaching your prospects at multiple touch points with multiple messages, fostering a relationship with them, to stay in touch with bypassing traditional media such as TV and print media, to deliver value directly over the web and to integrate a range of marketing activities into a seamless whole.

To make the most of what the internet can do for you, you need to develop an overall process flow that will guide you in coordinating your marketing activities. Such a process flow gives you clarity and lets you see things from a bird's eye-view.

Each business is different. Not all online marketing channels explained in this book will be applicable to you. It may so happen that some channels are more relevant than others. While email marketing may work for one business, it could be mobile marketing that brings more value to the other business. Choose a marketing mix that best suits the interests of your business.

The flowchart on the next page provides an idea of how various online marketing activities are linked together and drive your marketing machine. Now we will see how each process works.

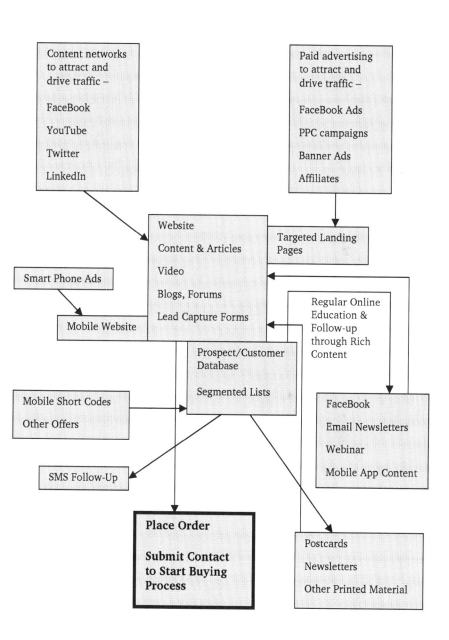

Set up your website and optimise it

Your website has to have a personality that best appeals to your buyers. The content, design, overall appeal, lead capture forms and the way the web pages correlate with the decision making cycle of buyers – all determine the success or failure you are going to have with online marketing.

All the traffic you attract could be under-exploited when the website and the content you present are not based on sound marketing fundamentals. The best sites are the ones that market your products and services to new customers, engage with existing customers and provide educating information to both.

Use paid advertising to attract traffic

Paid advertising platforms such as pay per click advertising, Face-Book ads, banner ads and affiliate marketing campaigns drive a lot of traffic even if you happen to be a novice on the web and the site is brand new.

Make sure that you optimise your landing pages to achieve high conversions. Understand that a home page has other objectives that make it difficult to achieve the same conversions as a specialised landing page.

Use content networks to drive traffic

Social media and social bookmarking sites are the best but probably the least utilised traffic generation tools when it comes to small business online marketing. A smart marketer would design and execute ongoing programs to identify potential customers and attract them with useful content via social media.

To see a substantial traffic coming from social networks may take some time but the effects are usually long-lasting – and free. Design engaging content that provides value to your customers and make it go viral on the web to attract traffic.

Use mobile marketing to stay in touch with your customers

Mobile marketing offers many possibilities, especially to small businesses. SMS, MMS, coupons, 2D bar codes, mobile URLs, common short codes, smartphone apps and location based targeting let you reach your customers in many ways. Make sure that you design a special mobile website that caters to the needs of visitors who access your site via mobile platforms.

Mobile marketing can be used for releasing short but useful information (restaurant booking, hotel reservation), commerce and billing, conducting polls and surveys, intimate special sales and discounts, overseeing supply chains and as a customer relationship management interface.

Manage your customer database and automate it

The not-so-secret drawback of many small businesses is that they don't pay the required attention toward nurturing leads. You need to have a sound lead capture strategy in place. Offer lead incentives such as free reports and white papers to attract leads. Use a marketing automation software application to manage contacts and follow them up with pre-designed content automatically.

Segmentation of your prospects and customers is very important. Separate warm leads from cold leads and target them with effective marketing messages. Similarly identify the customers to whom you can up-sell and cross-sell more products and services.

Educate your customers with rich content

Your conversation with a prospect does not end with a sale. You need to continue it by following up with content that is rich with information and has value. Write articles, send newsletters, provide them with white papers, form FaceBook communities and follow them up with offline marketing literature such as postcards and printed newsletters. This is probably the most difficult and time-consuming part but also the most important of all online marketing activities. This is an ongoing process and you need to have tenacity to keep it moving forward.

Doing it yourself

There are certain aspects of online marketing that are best left to professionals – website design, search engine optimisation, smartphone app design, etc. And the rest, you can do it on your own or develop skills with sufficient effort.

The most important skill you need, which you probably have but do not realise, is writing. Great content in a website is equivalent of a prime location in real estate. 97% of websites fail to thrive or remain mediocre because they lack hard hitting content. The rest attract traffic like magnets because they continuously provide information that is useful, interesting and appealing.

A lot of things in online marketing are free – blogs, social networking, email marketing and many software applications. But to make any real use of them you need to have or develop copywriting skills, marketing mindset and of course, lots of hard work.

Online marketing is not something you can dabble with for a week and then leave it just like that. It's not a one-time effort. Many small businesses spend a lot of time and money in building an alluring website that does not return anything but disappointment.

And then you see these smart entrepreneurs and small businesses who have built a strong online presence, astonishing personal brands and made a killing by turning themselves into internet celebrities. The internet offers an easy platform but to make it big you need to put in a lot of perseverance.

The internet offers many resources you can use to develop the skills you need. Be it copywriting or search engine optimisation or social media marketing – you can find almost a million guys teaching what they know and sharing their thoughts on the web. All you need to do is to spend some time, learn it bit by bit and put them into practice day in and day out.

It is an ongoing process

Online marketing needs regular investment of time and effort. Some things like building up backlinks, creating content, blogging, mobile optimisation, social bookmarking and social networking are ongoing processes. You need to keep on doing them to get the best results.

Perhaps the trickiest part of online marketing is creating new content that interests people. If you plan to do it yourself, then you need to brush up your writing skills and come up with appealing content that makes people come back to your site again and again. Another way is to hire copywriters and bloggers who will do these things for you, for a price, of course.

Plan for creating content

How do you plan to engage your audience? How do your audiences consume information? How frequently do they or how frequently do you want them to visit your site? What forms of content are most popular with your audience – articles, eBooks, white papers or podcasts? How does your content correlate with the buying decision-making process?

The above considerations will determine how frequently you should be creating content. Some content such as reports and white papers you intend to use as lead generation incentives should be prepared beforehand before launching marketing campaigns.

Some industries sell tangible products and do not need to discuss them regularly. They can create a volume of content and use it for marketing purposes. On the other hand, some industries which promote services, especially knowledge services, need to generate content on a regular basis.

Then there are blogs, surveys and email newsletters that need regular content creation. Plan to write newsletters or have them written at least one or two weeks prior to release. Blog posts, on the other hand, need to be up to date and discuss contemporary issues. Ideally you should at least blog once every week or two.

If you are an avid reader and are information-hungry, then you will have no problem finding topics to discuss and blog about them. If you plan to hire someone else, then you should clearly specify how frequently to blog and on what to blog.

Content is not just related to lead generation. You need something to continue the conversation even after closing a sale. No business can survive without repeat business. Think of how you can engage your past customers and how you can up-sell and cross-sell more products to them.

Plan events throughout the year

Every business has certain calendar events it can utilise to generate more leads and business. It could be the Christmas rush at the end of the year or summer discount sales or industry exhibitions.

Apart from that you also need to plan content that provides new information on a regular basis. Perhaps, you might want to add a new white paper every two months or offer an eBook every quarter.

Planning is also needed whenever you are about to kick-start special sales, discounts, promotions, product launches and product expansions. You need to develop the marketing communications material required to better take the news public via a host of marketing channels, both online and offline.

Use a calendar to plan updates in content on your website. You also need to inform your potential prospects and customers about the updates using various tools such as RSS, FaceBook community page, email notifications and mobile alerts.

Outsourcing your online marketing

Internet marketing is an ever-evolving discipline and the pace of change can be unsettling. To keep up with what happens in the online marketing and to do things on your own, you need to invest lots of time and effort. You need to be quick with learning new things and be good with a computer.

Many small business owners do not have the time and inclination to learn all this stuff and sort it out by themselves. As said earlier, to make it big on the internet on your own, you need to have lots of patience and perseverance.

Many successful internet entrepreneurs owe their success to the smart copywriters, SEO experts and web designers they keep around. If you plan to outsource your online marketing activities, then keep the following things in mind –

- Check their experience. This is, of course, obvious. Make sure that they know what they are talking about. Since many online marketing campaigns take time to produce results, you will be sticking around with these guys for a long time. So take care to pick the good guys.
- Strategy is something that cannot be outsourced. After all, no one understands your business more than you do. However, an effective online marketing company would bring in expertise and insights that help you put that strategy into action in the cyberspace.
- Talk to them about how online marketing impacts your business and how it can be integrated into your business systems and processes. Find out what ROI they can deliver. Ask for training and education they will provide to your employees.
- Don't get excited with jargon and buzzwords. Probe them about the returns on investment that can be realistically achieved with campaigns.
- Some companies offer blanket online marketing packages. You might not need all those services. Go for firms that offer a la carte services and let you pick the marketing mix and campaign structure.
- Look at the testimonials and if possible talk to former clients of the marketing company. Does this firm have a history of producing positive results for its clients? Does it form a long-term relationship with customers? How good are they at design and marketing? Do they focus on building eye-popping websites or simple but effective sites?
- When you choose an ongoing outsourcing online marketing partner, make sure that both the parties understand

the marketing strategy that is put in place. The marketing company also need to take care of ongoing campaigns and activities such as maintaining customer database, regular content creation, organic search engine optimisation and website updates.

Your online marketing action plan

An action plan provides a guideline to the overall online marketing process and helps you define measurable marketing objectives. Any new business looking to launch their website or an existing business set to kick-start a large online marketing campaign ought to have a marketing action plan.

The following sample action plan is in no way comprehensive and it does not profess to be one-size-fits-all template. Since every business is different and operates with different objectives and is in different stages of evolution, any action plan needs to be tailor-made to be effective.

The action plan or checklist given on the next few pages can offer you a basic idea of what an action plan has to be like. However, this is not a linear to-do list and a lot of things listed here must be performed concurrently and also on an ongoing basis to see significant results.

The strategy part

- Define your target audience
- Identify your strengths, weaknesses, opportunities and threats
- Develop a buyer's persona
- Identify the ways you can engage with that persona
- Detail your plan to reach your market
- Write down your vision
- Identify your marketing objectives
- Align your goals with the overall business goals
- Break your goals into measurable objectives
- Clearly espouse your value proposition
- Propose a detailed action plan

- Discuss it with your online marketing partner
- Devise a list of activities to be performed along with the timeline

Website design and development

- Build or redesign your website to suit your new marketing goals
- Maintain a balance between design objectives and marketing objectives
- Optimise the content for SEO
- Define your lead capture strategy
- Optimise the tags and meta descriptions of your web pages
- Design and optimise your landing pages
- Identify the content management system you wish to use
- Create a separate website for mobile users
- Set up a Google Analytics or similar analytics account
- Define your conversion goals and objectives
- Annotate important events in Google analytics
- Identify under-performing areas of your website and keep on optimising them

Search engine optimisation

- Set up your SEO tools
- Build your keyword lists
- Refine and identify your core organic search keywords
- Optimise your site and blog for the identified keywords
- Develop a time-line to build links
- Use SEO tools and analytics to track your progress
- Keep on adding content that attracts target audience

Content-driven traffic generation

- Start your company blog
- Submit your web pages to online directories
- Tag your articles and other content on social networking sites

- Bookmark your content on social media sites such as delicious
- Develop a timeline for your content generation activities
- Make your content on the site and blog shareable
- Write a special report, white paper and an eBook
- Post an online video
- Build at least three inbound links every week

Paid traffic generation

- Identify FaceBook opportunities
- Design FaceBook ads
- Track the progress of your FaceBook ads
- Create a FaceBook fan page for your site
- Create a Google AdWords account
- Create adverts based on your keywords
- Split your ads into groups
- Direct your traffic to special landing pages
- Create a separate landing page for each ad group
- Fine-tune your ads and pick the best one
- Use separate programs to achieve different marketing objectives
- Identify banner advertising opportunities
- Avoid banner ads if you do not find any juicy websites
- Create an account on affiliate networks
- Post information about your products on the network
- Identify top performing affiliates and approach them
- Actively go after the good affiliates instead of waiting for them

Lead generation

- Create a Feedburner or RSS account to notify your customers about new article and blog posts
- Identify the lead generation incentive such as a free special report or white paper or free 30-day trial
- Identify other stuff you wish to give away for free
- Define your traffic conversion goals
- Design the list of emails you want to target
- Buy marketing automation marketing software

- Plan the content you wish to send to your customers
- Pre-plan content for at least two months

Email marketing

- Create an appealing email template
- Automate your integrated database management application with the emails you wish to send to the leads
- Set up your drip campaign content delivery mechanism
- Segment your lists and keep on refining them
- Track, analyse and optimise your email campaigns

Mobile marketing

- Place a lead generation strategy in place and collect the phone numbers of your customers
- Integrate the data with your marketing automation application
- When there is an announcement to make send SMS or discount coupons or 2D bar codes to your prospects and customers
- Track and analyse their response
- Optimise your mobile marketing campaigns
- Set up mobile banner advertising account
- Set up mobile banner advertising campaigns

Social media marketing

- Define your brand and develop an online personality
- Create your accounts and profiles on Twitter, FaceBook, LinkedIn and other social media sites
- Build your YouTube channel and create videos
- Time your tweets and build a following
- Keep on posting new content on your blogs and site
- Bookmark your content on social networking sites
- Use sites like socialmarker.com to post your content on a host of other social media sites at once instead of logging on to each site
- Direct your traffic to targeted landing pages

Last Words

The internet is an exciting place to be. It changed the way we communicate with each other and also forced businesses to rethink the way they connect with their audience. It offers a wonderful platform for small businesses and entrepreneurs to express themselves creatively and compete with the big guys on a level playing field.

As they say in business, marketing is a conversation. And the internet is an amazing place to have conversations. Ultimately whether you fail or succeed in your online marketing campaigns depends how you make those conversations interesting and exciting.

We hope that this book served its purpose in educating you about how online marketing works and how you can use it to boost your business. We tried to be as simple as we can while explaining the concepts of internet marketing and avoiding use of jargon.

Many of the marketing strategies explained in this book have already been put to practice by hundreds of businesses who have achieved extraordinary results. While we understand that the road to realise your online marketing goals can be long and arduous, with patience, perseverance and smart strategies you can produce better business results. All the best.

About Better Business Results

Who We Are

Better Business Results, with offices in UK and Ireland, is a consultancy specialising in small and medium business systemisation, marketing and growth. We help businesses develop with proven online marketing techniques.

Better Business Results works with forward thinking business owners. We help them to facilitate fast growth and turn their businesses into money making vehicles that can be operated with less time commitment of the owner.

Better Business Results is accredited with the Better Business Institute (BBI) a global network of over 400 consultancies extensively trained in all areas of sales, marketing and business systematization.

What We Do

Better Business Results offers a range of digital marketing services that are proven and customisable. We understand different business owners have different styles or are at a different stage in their businesses.

Perhaps you are just starting out and have limited resources, if this is the case we have some great training and education resources to help you get going fast.

Maybe you are already successful and have a team in place to do your marketing, we can ensure you are getting the best from them and help you plan for the future.

A large number of our clients simply don't have the time and inclination to do their own marketing. They rely on us to do it for them while they reap the rewards

A La Carte Online Marketing Projects

Sometimes you need a helping hand just to get a specific project completed. We can help you with all manner of marketing tasks from setting up a new website to writing a press release.

Simply contact us with your requirements. We will give you a price and timeframe for completion. Then give us the nod and we will take care of it for you. Some of the things we can do for you are –

- Website design and development
- Mobile Optimised web sites
- Landing page creation
- Web Video production
- Brochure design and copywriting
- Sales letter copywriting
- Direct mail
- Advertisement design
- Email newsletter template design
- Printed newsletter template design
- White paper authoring
- Logo design and flyer design
- And much more

Ongoing Outsourced Marketing

Because every business is different we take the time to first understand what it is your business does, how you currently go about getting clients, and what your goals are for your business. From there we will review your current processes and marketing materials including your website and online presence.

Once we have done this we will then recommend some or more of the following:

- Create a complete marketing plan for you that forms the blueprint of all of the activities we will do for you and when.

- Executing the marketing plan and implementing everything.

- Setting up and managing your customer database system. The cornerstone of marketing your business is to keep good records of your leads and clients.

- Managing and updating your website including regular content creation and liaising with web developers.

- Ongoing marketing of your website using paid advertising and organic search engine optimisation.

Marketing Planning and Consultancy

Already have an in house marketing team? Not getting the results you hoped for? We will review your marketing and sales processes from the ground up and look at what you have done to date. We will then put together a detailed plan for your team to execute.

Our comprehensive 40 page marketing audit digs deep into your business and identifies areas which you may not have focused on in the past and which will provide the growth areas of the future.

Once the audit is complete we will put together a comprehensive Business Growth Blueprint which breaks down the opportunities within your business and details, step by step, what you need to do to take advantage of them.

Your Business Growth Blueprint isn't just about showing you how to get new clients, sure that's part of it, but there are other - equally (if not more) important and more cost effective - ways to grow your business.

Over the last few years we have perfected this system of analysing an existing business and implementing the correct techniques to maximise performance.

- Review your current marketing in depth

- Establish what is successful and what isn't

- Identify areas that can be improved

- Suggest new strategies for you to implement

Do-It-Yourself Marketing and Training

Often new businesses have limited resources and therefore are not able to afford to hire us to take care of their marketing for them. Also some business owners prefer to roll up their sleeves and do things themselves. If either of these statements describes you then we can still help you.

We have a number of training resources that you can access to give you the specifics to get a marketing task completed properly. Our marketing mastermind program is the best place to start if you are starting from scratch marketing a business.

Marketing Mastermind. This course is delivered online in a secure members' only area of our website. Each week you get access to new content that you can study and then apply to your business.

1. Key marketing training to keep you up to date
2. Varied course materials include video, audio, and printed worksheets to suit multiple learning styles
3. Step by step instructions on how to implement in your own business
4. Highly cost effective, low monthly subscription
5. Fits into any schedule and is suitable for any business

Social Media Blueprint. This is a 1 day course where delegates will learn how to harness social media to effectively market their business and connect with their customers. The course outline is as follows –

1. The social media landscape
2. The Dos and Don'ts of social media
3. Types of social media

4. Who am I trying to reach?
5. Do I really need social media?
6. Tracking your results for success
7. Creating a social media strategy for your business

Mobile Marketing. This is a 1 day course where delegates will learn how to harness mobile marketing to effectively market their business and connect with their customers. The course outline is as follows –

1. Understanding mobile marketing
2. Types of mobile marketing
3. Creating an effective SMS campaign
4. The ad platforms
5. Creating an app
6. Tracking your results for success
7. Creating a mobile marketing strategy for your business

To know more about how we can partner, please visit –

www.betterbusinessresults.com
Better Business Results
25, Straffan Gate, Straffan, Co. Kildare, Ireland
Phone: Ireland +353 (0) 1 488 0985, UK +44 (0)20 8242 4045
Email: info@betterbusinessresults.com

About the Author

Matt has worked as a Business Analyst and IT consultant for over 9 years with a number of large organisations including Bear Stearns, AIB, Pioneer Investments and Hewlett Packard. He has also owned and operated a number of successful enterprises.

Through all of his endeavours the common denominator was a realisation that for businesses to be successful they needed to systemise their marketing and other operations.

Matt has spent a number of years studying and implementing the techniques of Jay Abraham, Dan Kennedy, Gary Halbert, Peter Sun, Bill Myers and Michael E. Gerber.

When not working, Matt enjoys spending time with his wife and 3 children.

Matt's specialist skills include –

- Setting up a sales process
- Direct response Copywriting
- Implementing lead generation and follow up systems
- Establishing Business Development Programs for SMEs
- Digital Marketing
- Project Management

21200107R00088

Made in the USA
Charleston, SC
11 August 2013